Child Marriage in India: Issues and Challenges

Child Marriage in India: Issues and Challenges

A.K. Kakkar

CYBER TECH PUBLICATIONS
4264/3, Ansari Road, Daryaganj, New Delhi-110002 (India)
Ph.: 011-23244078. Fax: 011-23280028
E-Mail: cyberpublicationsdelhi@yahoo.com

CHILD MARRIAGE IN INDIA: ISSUES AND CHALLENGES

A.K. Kakkar

First Edition 2009

Published by :

G.S. Rawat for **Cyber Tech Publications**
4264/3, Ansari Road, Daryaganj, New Delhi-110002 (India)
Ph.: 011-23244078. Fax: 011-23280028
E-Mail: cyberpublicationsdelhi@yahoo.com

Printed at : .

Preface

Along with the freedom struggle which was for the realisation of the human rights of the people of India to live in freedom and dignity, a process of social reform was also underway to bring women and disadvantaged sections of society into the mainstream. Both these processes converged and found expression in the Indian Constitution which came into effect in 1950, less than three years after gaining independence. The forward looking Constitution embodies the very essence of the freedom struggle and is reflective of the ethos of pluralism and tolerance engendered by a multi-religious, multi-cultural, multi-lingual and multi-ethnic society.

The commitment to pluralism and tolerance continues and informs all aspects of the Indian Constitution. The Indian Constitution is one of the longest in the world and drew inspiration not only from the richness of our experience of assimilating many religions and cultures over the millennia, but also the leading democratic constitutions of the modern world and from the fledgling United Nations.

India, with a population of around 350 million at the time of independence in 1947, faced stupendous challenges. There were nearly 600 Princely States in addition to those areas known as British India which had to be integrated. The Indian economy was primarily an agrarian economy which was deficient in industries and dependent on imports for its basic needs. The literacy rate was around 18 per cent. In the first few decades, priority was given to building human and industrial capacity in keeping with the needs and priorities of the nation. This was the setting against which India began its journey as a democracy to ensure the basic political, economic, social and cultural rights of her people.

—Author

Preface

CONTENTS

1

CHILD MARRIAGE IN INDIA

Child marriage was a common feature in India before Indian Independence in 1947. After Independence, child marriages have been made illegal. The legal age to marry in India is set at 18 for women and 21 for men. The law is followed in most parts of India but in some regions of the country parents arrange child marriages for their children. Children as young as 10 years old are married off in the states of Rajasthan.

In an effort to curb the practice of child marriages the states of Rajasthan, Gujarat, Maharashtra, Karnataka and Himachal Pradesh in India have passed laws that mandate the registration of all marriages in order to make it a valid marriage.

But mass marriages that involve children are frequently ignored by authorities. According to a 1991 census, Rajasthan was the state with the most child marriages.

INDIA'S EFFORT TO STOP CHILD MARRIAGE HITS A WALL

While India has been waging a campaign against the traditional practice of child marriage, many people here consider it a failed, half-hearted effort. The government's defeat has been symbolized by the image of Shakuntala Verma, a 48-year-old social worker who lies in a hospital, both arms crudely severed above the wrists. Verma believes her limbs were slashed by a local villager, angry at the work -she was doing in rural Madhya Pradesh, a state in central India, to prevent about 20 child weddings from going ahead.

"I'd been visiting families in the village, going into their homes and trying to persuade them against marrying their children," she said. Calm and articulate, as she recuperated after a 16-hour operation to rejoin arteries, bones, veins and nerves, she explained: "I wasn't welcomed by the villagers. Parents hid their children and lied about their ages. There was a lot of anger about my presence there. I'm quite certain that the attack was connected to the work I was doing."

Eager to improve its poor record on child marriage, the state government increased pressure on its grassroots social workers this year, demanding that they take greater responsibility for underage marriages.

Verma was given a list of local families who were thought to be planning weddings for their children on May 11, an auspicious day for marriage. She spent 10 days trying to explain to the locals why this could prove harmful to their children.

"The youngest child was 10, but the average age was around 15 or 16," she said. "Although the parents were not willing to listen, I kept trying to explain to them that we wanted to help the children have a better future. The response was not very good."

Verma was at home alone on the eve of planned ceremonies in Bhangadh, a remote village in the west of the state. The children had already been anointed with ceremonial dabs of tumeric, a final preparation for marriage. A man she did not recognize arrived and hacked at her head and arms with a knife, leaving her hands hanging by threads of skin and flesh. The police say there is no firm evidence to connect the attack with the issue of child marriage.

Nevertheless, Verma's case has been the trigger for an analysis of why the government is failing in its mission to combat the countryside's adherence to early marriage.

Statistics are elusive, but estimates are that 40 to 50 percent of marriages in India involve a girl under 18 or a boy under 21, the legal ages for marriage.

According to Unicef, 82 percent of girls in Rajasthan, where the practice is particularly widespread, are married by 18; 15 percent of girls in rural areas across the country are married before 13; and 52 percent of girls have their first pregnancy between 15 and 19.

Child support agencies catalogue the dire consequences that follow early marriage, particularly for girls: The child's education is sacrificed; girls become more vulnerable to domestic violence and are weakened by early pregnancies; and babies born to girls under 17 are 60 percent are more likely to die during their first year of life. Unicef describes child marriage as a "gross violation of all categories of child rights."

The government appears unwilling to crack down on the practice with any great energy, however, and its ambivalence toward the issue is echoed with equal lethargy at every level.

"People have never taken this issue very seriously," said Jaya Sagade, the author of "Child Marriage in India," published this year by Oxford University Press. "No political party has taken proper action against it; neither has anyone in the legal fraternity. There's a sense that it won't be possible to uproot such an entrenched custom."

The law itself is weak. Parents can theoretically be sentenced to three months' imprisonment, but they very rarely are; a survey in 2001 found that there were never more than 89 attempted prosecutions across India in any one year. Although the act of marrying children is against the law, the marriage itself is valid once performed, even if the child was as young as 5 at the time. The police do not have the authority to arrest anyone about to take part in a marriage, and the bureaucracy involved in preventing one is so complicated that most weddings have already gone ahead by the time the papers are ready.

Premlal Pandey, the inspector general of the police in the Indore region, where Verma was attacked, said his officers were reluctant to interfere.

"We have limited manpower, so we have to decide where the thrust of policing should be," he said. "Mostly we choose to be active in the criminal field. If we intervene in child marriages, we get enemies; relatives get extremely angry. Legally, we may be correct, but we are not welcomed by society because most people do not consider this to be an evil. "We can't arrest people, so the only choice is to use force. What does force mean? Well, violence. Yes, beating. It's extremely difficult."

For every argument that child-welfare agencies produce, parents have a counterclaim: it makes economic sense to marry off all the girls in one family in order to avoid the cost of multiple weddings; finding a husband swiftly for a girl removes the burden of feeding and educating her; and marriage relieves parents of the responsibility of preserving a girl's honor throughout adolescence.

Some parents argue that girls who are married off very young are not dispatched to the husband's family before puberty, an argument Sagade dismissed.

"Even if it's true that the girl remains at home until reaching puberty-which I don't believe is usually the case-puberty is usually around 12 or 13, which is still far too young to be ending childhood," Sagade said.

A HISTORY OF CHILD MARRIAGE IN INDIA

Mother: I will cut off your ears.

Daughter: Oh, I will see how you cut off my ears.

Mother: Really, I am telling you, I will cut off your ears and send them to the mill, and they will make flour and we will have bread from that.

Daughter: Don't be silly.

Introduction: The Reform Movement 1860-1886

In India during the 1860's, marriage meant girls getting married below 8 or 9 years old. Socio-reform religious movements such as the Brahmo Samaj and the Arya Samaj pioneered work against child marriage. Late in the 1860's some success was met when the Indian Penal Code prohibited intercourse with a wife who had not reached ten years of age.

Nevertheless, it wasn't until 1880 that child marriage as a problem became a public issue in India during the debate on the Age of Consent Bill. Towards the end of the debate a child wife of eleven years old, Named Phulmani, died when her husband raped her. More than 500 women doctors sent a memorandum to the Viceroy requesting him to stop marriage of girls below 14 years of age. The resulting bill compromised at 12 years old.

On August 15, 1884 a Parsee reformist, Behramji Malabari, circulated two notes which highlighted the evils of child marriage and enforced widowhood. The Honorable J. Gibbs added his comments to Malabari's notes saying that, "Young mothers become stunted in growth, and often become invalids for life, while children were too often pony and weak." Kadhavdas added to the list of evils, "Early marriage is a great obstacle in the progress of female education."

Shortly thereafter, in 1886 the first petition against 'Hindu Infant Marriage' was proposed to the Government by the natives of Meerut. It was finally passed in 1927. It declared that no marriage would be valid unless the girl had completed her twelfth year. In spite of laws prohibiting the practice, child marriage continues to be a widespread custom in India. After looking at the debate which raged in the 1880's, I look at Hindu scriptures and their mandates for the practice.

THE MALABARI LETTERS-1887

Between 1884 and 1887 Behramji Malabari collected opinions for and against infant marriage and enforced widowhood from "representative Hindu gentlemen and official and other authorities." The "Hindu gentlemen" were mostly selected from Brahmins educated in English universities. The resultant letters, dedicated to the Duke and Duchess of Connaught were published in the Voice of India. Malabari argued that infant marriage was "a practice more evil than infanticide." His arguments against infant marriage can be summarized as a too early consummation of the nuptial troth, breaking down the constitutions and the ushering in of disease, the birth of sick children, the necessity of feeding too many mouths, poverty and dependence, and a disorganized household leading perhaps to sin.

A response by Ramanujchari's typifies the reformer's view of child marriage, an evil which he thought that even the reformers were unaware, ".the practice of the selling of girls by their parents. has become so rife in these parts of the country that girls are disposed of in marriage to the highest bidders like goods at an auction sale. Girls are married, as a rule, before they attain their 8th or 9th birthday-an age when they are utterly incompetent to comprehend the contract they enter into." The authors included in Malabari's publication nearly universally condemned infant marriage as a "great physical and moral evil." Infant marriage was considered "one of two evils that, if not remedied in time, are sure to destroy the vitality of the whole native community of India." Infant marriage was not confined to the Hindus, but was also "practiced by Parsis and Mohamedans."

Two related issues were being discussed, child marriage and infant widowhood. Shirgaonkar, not so interested in child marriage, objected to child widowhood. He said, "I condemn infant marriages not because I think that they afterwards prove unhappy-which statement I will not accept unsupported by statistics-but because such marriages increase infant widows"

How child marriage works to increase infant widows and their misery is hinted at by Colonel E.W. West, "I have known many cases of old men marrying girls not yet emerged from childhood and it needs but little knowledge of human nature to realize the misery during the husband's lifetime, and of Hindu ways to realize the misery after his death, of the girl."

Many authors felt that government action was a necessity: "The reason for this is that for the last 2000 years the Hindoos have lost the power of refection, and even that of following or imitating what is good.. The masses still grope in darkness. They are bound by their customs and the foolish teachings of their priests."

Of the eighty-seven respondents, only a few suggested that the evil wasn't as great as Malabari considered it to be. For example, Dr. Rajendralala Mitra from Calcutta said, "I have also yet to learn that disparity in age of marriage does more harm in India than it does in Europe."

Mozoomdar objected and offered some statistics, arguing that the problem of infant widowhood wasn't nearly so serious as propounded. According to the census there were only 28,369 widows between the ages of 14 and 19 out of twenty million total widows in India.

More than a few of the respondents objected to Malabari's proposal for prohibition of child marriage. Taleyarkhanfrom Baroda argued that, "Our English ideas actually jar with their (the Hindus) sympathies, the antipathies, and all important affections of their heart and mind."

He goes on to explain that that 'marriage seasons' can be at intervals as many as twelve years apart. In the case cited a girl of four couldn't be married until she was sixteen, "A horrible purgatory, according to the Shastras, for the parents to keep her unmarried at that age."

He continues by saying, "It is a wonder how this nation has succeeded for ages in preserving such a marked harmony of their homes. If we have weakly children the homes are happy, contented, well regulated and economical."

REFORMERS IGNORED HINDU SCRIPTURES AND EPICS

Malabari claims that, "No Shastra enforces marriage proper on a girl under 12 years of age, when presumably the boy must be between 15 and 20." That being Malabari's only comment on the religious basis of the nearly universal custom of child marriage he concluded, "So much as to the social or so-called religious aspect of the practice."

The writers who supported Malabari, with one or two exceptions, also denied the religious-spiritual background of infant marriage. Lakshmiram, for example, said, "There is one foolish text, I know, which enjoins the marriage of every girl before she is eleven years old."

One exception to this denial is found in the letter of Keshaveal Madhavadas who says, "The Hindu law gives clear injunction not to keep a girl unmarried beyond 12 years old." While it does appear to be arguable that the Vedic literature, written before 400 B.C. advised that children not be married before puberty, in the following compilation I show that the British and their Brahmin supporters ignored the long Hindu scriptural tradition of child marriage during Vedic times and after the fourth century BC. The citations also help us understand the point of view of a civilization that allowed for child marriage.

Child Marriage Before the Fourth Century B.C.

The Vedic mantras, such as the Rigveda mentioned that a girl could be married only when she was fully developed both physically and mentally and that she was to be fully developed physically before leaving her father's home. Men were advised to marry a girl with a fully developed body. One hymn mentions that a female should be married only "when she is not a child". One modern commentator, Sharma who wrote in 1993, argues that during the time of the great epics, the Ramayana and Mahabharata, the girls "used to be grown up at the time of marriage".

Sharma's reasoning is that, "In the Ramayana it is described that the brides came to Ayodhya and after paying due respect to the elders lived merrily with their husbands in seclusion which presupposes post-puberty marriages." Sharma also argues that the marriage rituals described in the Grihyasutras, the Baudhayana presuppose that the marriageable age was after puberty. The consummation of the marriage could take place directly after the marriage ceremonies or a few days afterwards. "Since consummation couldn't possibly take place before puberty," goes Sharma's reasoning, the bride must have reached maturity. It sounds as if Sharma considers pre-pubescent girls as being physically incapable of having intercourse and therefore not marriageable.

Malabari, more than century before Sharma, discussed the ability of pre-pubertal girls to consummate marriage willingly when he wrote A.O. Hume, "Mr. Hume is informed that consummation is deferred in many cases. Not so to my knowledge.it takes but little knowledge of human nature to see that infant marriage super-induces precocious development in the case of the boy. In the case of the girl it is worse, and almost all circumstances conspire to make her a willing accessory to what, on public grounds, I am constrained to denounce as a crime." According to Malabari, pre-pubescent sexual relationships while both common and consensual, were still a "crime".

Also suggestive that the Rigveda allowed for child marriage is a hymn that mentions that Indra gave a child-wife named Vrichaya to the old man Kashivan. Furthermore, in the epic Aranyakanda, the godess Sita is supposed to have told Ravana that when she was kidnapped by him, she was eighteen and her husband twenty five and that they had spent twelve years at Ayodhya. From this commentary, the age of Sita is known to have been six years old at the day of her marriage. Sharma (1993) argued this is not true because, "the Ramayana was recast many times and the verses in question are from later editions." He says the same concerning the Uttararamacharita Bhavabhuti which described Sita as a child bride playing at the knee of her mother-in-law.

Only in the Mahabharta is there a unequivocable injunction that a girl should be married after puberty. In fact this work decrees that she should wait three years after puberty to obtain a husband.

The Kamasutra on Courtship

The Kama Sutra is attributed to Vatsyayana who wrote his "profound discussion of love and sex" no later than 300 AD and perhaps as early as 300 BC. The work wasn't original, it was a summing up of ancient wisdom. Love and sex were considered as something a-moral, something which transcends ethics and has its own justifications.

According to the Kama Sutra the results of marrying a young girl is untarnished love, "When a girl of the same cast, and a virgin, is married in accordance with the precepts of the Holy Writ (Darma Shastras), the results of such a union are. untarnished love."

Loving a girl that had been loved by others would be reproachful, "But at all events, says Ghotakamukha, a girl who has already been joined with others (that is, no longer a maiden) should never be loved, for it would be reproachful to do such a thing." A girl who has "fully arrived at puberty" should be avoided as a wife.

The Kama Sutra describes wooing, "When a boy has thus begun to woo a girl that he loves, he should spend his time with her and amuse her with various games and diversions fitted for their age and acquaintanceship, such as picking and collecting flowers, making garlands of flowers, playing parts of members of a fictitious family.. the game of odds and evens, the game of finding out the middle finger, the game of six pebbles. Hide-and-seek, playing with seeds, blind-man's bluff and other games of the same sort." In short, child's games.

If the wooer is a man he should, "attach himself to the daughter of the girl's nurse and. procure for her such playthings as may be hardly known to other girls. He should give her dolls made of cloth.."

We may wonder what the girl thinks of all this. According to the Kama Sutra, a girl always shows her love by outward signs and actions, "She never looks the man in the face and becomes abashed when she is looked at by him; under some pretext or another she shows her limbs to him; she looks secretly at him; hangs down her head when she is asked some questions by him, and answers in indistinct words and unfinished sentences, delights to be in his company for a long time; under some pretext or another she makes him look at different things, narrates to him tales and stories very slowly so that she may continue conversation with him for a long time; always wears anything that he may have presented to her, and becomes dejected when any other bridegroom is mentioned by her parents.."

That the attentions are being paid to pre-pubescent girls is shown clearly by the concluding paragraph on Kama Sutra courtship, "A man who has seen and perceived the feelings of the girl toward him, and who has noticed the outward signs and movements by which those feelings are expressed, should do everything in his power to effect a union with her. He should gain over a young girl by childlike sports."

Later, in the Yajñvalkya Smriri and its contemporary literature, we find that the fear of post-puberty marriages became so great that the Smitris brought the marriageable age of girls still lower. According to the Parashar Smitri and Sheeghrabodha the marriageable girls were divided into five categories:

(1) Nagnika or naked. A girl seven years old or younger. This was regarded as best age for marriage.

(2) Gauri. A girl eight years old.

(3) Rohini. A girl of nine years old.

(4) Kanya. A ten years old girl.

(5) Rajaswala. A girl above ten years old.

According to Vaikhnasa, a Brahmin should marry a Nagnika since that is the best match. According to Marici the best age of marriage for a girl is five years old. Brahmapurana also prescribes marriage in childhood.

Failure to do this will condemn the parents or gaurdian to utmost degradation.

Child Marriage from the 6th Century AD-1400 AD

After the sixth century the marriageable age of girls went down lower and lower. The stoppage of participation of girls in Vedic education, Upanayana rituals and the insistence of purity in yajna (sacrificial) ritual contributed to the lowering of the marriage age for girls.

All the literature of the epic clearly show the tendency to lower the age of marriage age of girls. The injunction in the Dharmasutra for a woman to wait three years after obtaining womanhood to select a mate was limited to three months by Guatama and Vishnu. Guatama said that a girl should be married before she attains womanhood, otherwise it would be a sin. According to the Baudhayana and Vashithat Dharmasutras a father who allowed his daughter to remain unmarried until after her first menstruation was considered guilty of the sin of abortion on each monthly period.

Later, the Manusmitri places stress on the suitability of the groom and makes it clear that marriage of a girl before her first menstruation was permissible. In the Baudhayana it is said that a girl should be given in marriage to a suitable groom even if she is immature, and that if she is mature she should be given in marriage even if the groom is unsuitable.

By the time of the Yajnavalkyasmitri and its contemporary literature, we find that the fear of post-puberty marriage became so great that the marriageable age was brought down even lower. Nagnika, girls seven years old or younger, were regarded as the best by Vaikknasa. Marichi considered the best age for marriage of girls to be five years old. It was said that if a father does not give her girls in marriage, then the ancestors of the girl would drink the menstrual flow of the girl.

The Ratirimanjeri of Jayadeva-1400 AD

About 1000 years (1400-1500 AD) after the Kamasutra, the Ratimañjari or "The Posy of Love' described the 125 slokas, or sexual positions. The work was dedicated to Lord Siva.

Young girls are mentioned in only two verses, Until sixteen years, a young girl was called bala, until thirty she was called taruni, or young woman. The Ratimañjari said, "The bala is a lover of flowers and sweet things, the young woman is given to love-play. The bala gives a man pleasure and the breath of life, prana; the taruni draws out the breath of life."

An allusion is made to hairlessness as being attractive. "Now the queynt of woman should be like the back of a tortoise, the cassia blossom, lotus-scented, hairless and well spread: these five are accounted desirable.

The Koka Shastra-1400 AD

The Koka Shastra also discusses courtship with young girls. "The bala can be won by giving betal fruit, promising her elaborate meals, by recounting all manner of wonders to her, by the arts and by games."

Young girls or young girl somatypes are preferred sexual partners, "A pretty girl of phlegmatic constitution; a mare- or gazelle-woman, yaksi, human or goddess-type; a young girl or one in the freshness of youth-this is the ideal for those who desire pleasure in the world."

In another verse we find that, "A young girl from a strange part of the country should be studied accordingly: her inborn inclinations can be found only from experience.. When you have considered this discrepancy between individual preference and local custom, and also somatype, speed of reaching orgasm, degree of response, age group, and constitutional type, you -can proceed accordingly-first to appropriate 'outer forms'-the first of these are the embrace..Until her sixteenth year a girl is called bala a young girl who is not yet mature must be approached by way of the 'outer' forms of lovemaking."

The outer forms of love-making include embraces. There are two sorts of embrace for those who have not yet declared their love, four embraces by which they can make known their mind, and eight embraces for those who have shared love-pleasure already.

Children are to avoided for the inner form of love-making, as we can see from the following verse, "Woman who has been put out of her caste, a personal friend, a child, an invalid, a woman who makes love in public, a lunatic, or one who is ill-smelling, aged are always to be avoided as a matter of practice".

More Hindu Scriptual Sources-Nineteenth Century Opinions

Hindu religion enjoined parents not to keep a girl unmarried even at as small an age as 8 years. Puberty sets in among Indian females generally after 11 years, when any marriage is considered unholy. Jayal said that, "Hindu law gives clear injunction not to keep a girl unmarried beyond 12 years."

Keeping girls unmarried until their first menstruation would condemn the family to hell, as Paitinashi said, "A damsel should be given in marriage before her breasts swell. But if she has menstruated before marriage, both the giver and the taker fall into the abyss of hell; and her father, grandfather, and great grandfather are born insects in ordure."

In addition, Brahmins who married girls after their first period would become outcastes as spoken of in the Angirasmitri where it is said, "There is no atonement for man who has intercourse with a Vrishali, i.e, a woman who has her courses before marriage. It is also stated, ". the father, mother and elder brother who tolerate a girl in her courses before marriage go to hell.. A Brahmin who will marry such a girl is not to be spoken of or admitted to society."

Hindu scriptures sanctioned both child marriage and early consummation, "the girl should be married before puberty and certainly immediately after her first menstruation. If a girl gets married after her first menses it would not be a Kanya-dan but stree-dan". Kanya-dan can be consummated at the most at 11 years of her age." In one of the scenes in the Shastras a father addresses his father-in-law on giving her in marriage, "I have brought this girl up for eight years like a boy. I now give her away to your son, treat her with affection." (Nagi 1993:4).

Age at Marriage

The Manu, Mahabharata and the Vishnu Purana decreed that the man should be three times older than the girl, thus a man marrying a ten year old should be thirty, an eight year old girl should marry a man of twenty-four and so on. One pragmatical Hindu reformer suggested that a law be made prohibiting the marriage of a man over the age of 45 with a girl younger than twelve.

The practice of marrying girls between the age of two and eight years old was common, not only amongst the Hindus, but the Mohammedans and Parsees. Even the Prophet of Islam married a child as a first wife. Oman (No date) complained that, "it is undeniably true that throughout India the marriage of very young girls from 2 to 8 years old of age, with equally young boys, or often with adults of any age, is a very common practice amongst Hindus. The practice also prevails in lesser degrees amongst Parsees and Indian Muhammadans, but it cannot be repugnant to the religious sentiments of the later, since the Prophet of Islam married Ayishah when she was nine years old. She was his favorite wife, and lived to the age of sixty-nine." Abielle (No date) found that child marriage was prevalent even in the Christian areas of India. One of Abielle's more interesting findings was that their was a near unanimity of satisfaction of the couples involved with their experiences in child marriage.

As for consummation Oman continues, "Equally true it is that even consummation of marriage has commonly taken place when the child-wife is perhaps not more than ten years of age."

Discussion

The East India Company's 17th century "looting spree" turned into a permanently profitable business by the 1800's. The British Prime Minister Salisbury soberly decreed that India should be bled "judiciously". A flood of Christian preachers, missionaries and teachers were dispatched to Anglicize the "savages." While appearing to be judicious, they were vicious in their derision of Hindus and their customs. The Brahmin caste were eager for social acceptance by those in power and quick to adopt European ideas. According to the social historian Amrit Srinivasan, "Civilizing the Indians through enforcing a uniform adoption of the Victorian ethic for women" became a central goal of the reformers. Gradually the seeds of cultural shame were sown and an Indian clone of British mentality successfully bred. From then onwards, the most effective critics of Hindu tradition were Indians themselves.

The English, who were ignorant of the long tradition of Indian spiritual literature, declared that there was no religious basis for child marriage and found support for their beliefs from their supporters within the Brahmin caste. Nearly all British educated Indians of the era parroted the English position that child marriage was an insidious evil and destroying the fabric of Indian society.

The Indian populace disagreed. As K.N. Kane of Bombay said in 1884, "There cannot be two opinions about the evil effects which these customs produce in Hindu society, but the efforts of both high and low have been rendered futile owing to the majority of the Hindu population adhering tenaciously to the opposite views." If Kane is to believed, the majority of India's people thought child marriage to be beneficial and a source of pride. Larkshmiram, who considered child marriage a "curse", also said that, "The common saying, 'my children were betrothed while in the cradle yet' is the proud expression of the completely satisfied aspiration of a Gujurato parent."

At the time of the British reform movement in the 1880's scholars and politicians reported girls being married at 8 and 9 years old to men three times their age, an ancient Hindu, and apparently Mohammadan and Parsee custom. The practice of marrying girls before they were thirteen was all but universal. According to various authors many of the marriages were consummated before puberty. Malabari himself said that, "The nuptial ceremonies, I think, are a direct inducement in 95 out of 100 cases to a too early consummation. Even the utmost precaution taken by sensible parents fails to keep the pair from mischief." The English called them "victims". Anglicized Hindus called them "willing victims in the vast majority of cases."

Cross-generation marriage was both sanctioned and encouraged by at least two thousand years of scripture and literature, perhaps even longer if we accept that Sita was a "child-bride at the knee of her mother-in-law."

An unmigated evil as the English believed? Or beneficial as the Hindus believed? Shirgaonkar, would not accept that child marriages were unhappy and complained of a lack of statistics. Taleyarkhan noted Hindu families as "happy, contented, well regulated and economical." Former Government Secretary to India, Allan Octavian Hume who almost single-handedly establish the Indian National Congress told Malabari, "I must say that I think that you somewhat exaggerate the evil results of these traditional institutions. There are millions of cases in which early marriages are believed to be daily proving happy ones."

Hume quotes a letter from a native friend, "Those ignorant of our inner life calls this a vile subjugation and say that we have made our wives our slaves, but those who live amongst us know, that it is the result of that deep seated affection that springs from early association. Where will you find a wife as true and contented as the Hindu women of a respected family?"

CHILD MARRIAGES, THOUGH ILLEGAL, PERSIST IN INDIA

If a wedding is supposed to fulfill a girl's earliest dreams, Hansa's in this tiny hamlet in Rajasthan state seemed more like a nightmare.

Early in the starlit evening, the smoke from the sacred fire began searing her eyes. The rituals pushed the ceremony deep into the night, in a crucible of heat and haze. After the first two hours, Hansa was quietly sobbing. By midnight, with Hindu priests leading Hansa and her new husband, Sitaram, in the climactic ritual, involving seven purifying circuits of the wood-burning fire, Hansa's wailing was drowning the rhythmic mantras of the priests.

"I want to go to bed," she cried. "Please, Mama, Papa. Let me sleep!"

Bafflement can only have worsened the ordeal, since Hansa, the youngest of six sisters being married in a joint ceremony to boys from-other villages, was only 4. Her husband was 12.

Such weddings are common in Rajasthan, a state known for its desert landscapes, hilltop forts and maharajahs' palaces, as well as its persistence in feudal traditions, including child marriages, that have kept Rajasthani women among the most socially disadvantaged in India.

Indian law sets 18 as the minimum age for a woman to marry and 21 for a man. When India's Parliament adopted the Child Marriage Restraint Act in 1978, legislators hoped that the statute would curb child marriages and the social ills they perpetuate.

Concern focused on an arc of populous northern states where child marriages are most deeply rooted: Rajasthan, Madhya Pradesh, Uttar Pradesh, Bihar and West Bengal, with a combined population of 420 million, about 40 percent of all Indians.

According to decades of research, child marriages contribute to virtually every social problem that keeps India behind in women's rights. The problems include soaring birth rates, grinding poverty and malnutrition, high illiteracy and infant mortality, and low life expectancy, especially among rural women. In Rajasthan, a survey of more than 5,000 women conducted by the national government in 1993 showed that 56 percent had married before they were 15. Of those, 3 percent married before they were 5 and another 14 percent before they were 10. Barely 18 percent were literate, and only 3 percent used any form of birth control other than sterilization.

Large families and poor health for children and mothers were among the results. The survey showed that of every 1,000 births, 73 children died in infancy, and 103 were under the age of 5 when they died. Sixty-three percent of children under 4 were found to be severely undernourished. Average life expectancy for women was 58.

In every case, the figures were among the worst for any Indian state.

Social workers report that many husbands tire of their marriages after the third, fourth or fifth child, when their wives are still teen-agers. Alcoholism contributes to domestic violence, with sometimes fatal beatings.

In some cases, husbands sell their wives, and even their unmarried daughters, as sexual partners to other men. In scores of cases every year, village women strike back by killing their husbands, only to face long terms in prison.

"It is a tragedy for these little flowers, and for our country, that they are snatched away into marriage before they even have a chance to bloom," said Mohini Giri, 60, chairwoman of the National Commission for Women, a government agency established in the early 1990s that has become a driving force for raising awareness about the plight of women.

In Rajasthan, child marriages remain so popular that virtually every city, town and village takes on a holiday atmosphere ahead of the day set by astrologers for the annual Akha Teej festival--the moment judged most auspicious for marriages.

On the day of the festival, usually in late April or early May, roads are choked with tractors pulling trailers filled with gaily dressed wedding guests. On the outskirts of every settlement there are open-sided wedding tents in brightly patterned fabrics known as pandals.

Each year, formal warnings are posted outside state government offices stating that child marriages are illegal, but they have little impact.

Three strangers arriving at Madhogarh, the village where Hansa was married, had only to pull off the main road running south from the town of Alwar, 125 miles southwest of New Delhi, and drive a mile to spot a wedding pandal.

Villagers were unhesitating in their welcome, even when one of the visitors was introduced as a reporter.

"Of course, we know that marrying children is against the law, but it's only a paper law," said Govind Singh Patel, a village elder in the cattle-herding Gujjar community, which is among the poorest in Rajasthan and the most resistant to social change.

Sociologists say the Gujjars and similar groups trace the origin of child marriages to Muslim invasions that began more than 1,000 years ago. Legend has it that the invaders raped unmarried Hindu girls or carried them off as booty, prompting Hindu communities to marry off their daughters almost from birth to protect them.

Today, the stories have an echo in the local view that any girl reaching puberty without getting married will fall prey to sexual depredations, some from men imbued with the common belief that having sex with a "fresh" girl can cure syphilis, gonorrhea and other sexually transmitted diseases, including AIDS.

Tradition has been reinforced by necessity. In villages like Madhogarh, a family can be fortunate to have an annual income of $500, less in years when there is drought or flood. Securing early marriages for daughters can mean the difference between subsistence and hunger. Traditionally, this has meant seeking grooms in neighboring villages, since the fear of inbreeding has generated a taboo against marriage between boys and girls from the same village.

Hansa's father, Shriram Gujjar, 40, works an acre of land beside the family's thatched home of mud and straw, with three cows to supplement his crop of mustard and wheat. Villagers say his troubles were compounded when his wife, Gyarsi Devi, gave birth to seven daughters but-no sons.

But Gujjar's fortunes improved when a network of community contacts found husbands for the first six daughters, ranging in age from 4-year-old Hansa to Dohli, 14. An infant girl of 18 months, and another child on the way, will await another marriage ceremony in the future.

Gujjar, a fierce-looking man with a handlebar mustache and a luxuriant white turban, said he had borrowed about 60,000 rupees, about $1,500, to pay for the dowries required by the grooms' families and for the wedding festivities. While the loan will be a problem for years, he said, the weddings mean that he can now look forward to growing old without being trapped in penury by the need to support his daughters.

"Tonight I am a free man again!" he said, grinning as he circulated proudly among the scores of wedding guests seated cross-legged beneath the pandal.

After a moment to check the register in which cash donations from the guests were being entered, he returned, thrust his hands into the air in a gesture of release and added, "Thanks to God, the heaviest of my burdens has been lifted."

The brides spend the night of their weddings in their homes, and then join their husband's families the next day for a journey to their in-laws' village.

In Hansa's case, this entailed traveling half a day by oxcart and bus to a village 25 miles away. After a few days there, tradition required that she return to her family in Madhogarh and await the onset of puberty, when another ceremony known as the Gauna would mark her fitness to join her husband's family. But not all grooms' families are prepared to wait for puberty. In many cases documented by sociologists, girls as young as 6 or 7 have been taken away by their husbands' families to begin working as servants or field hands.

"With the addition of a girl to the household, the in-laws get a laborer, someone who will feed the cattle and clear the house, a servant who comes free of cost," said Ratan Katyani, a social worker in the Rajasthan city of Jaipur.

In 1994 the National Commission for Women urged the national government, then headed by Prime Minister Narasimha Rao, to consolidate the separate marriage laws that exist for each of the major religious communities--Hindu, Muslim and Christian--and to include a provision requiring that all marriages be legally registered. That, the commission reasoned, could be used to bar any under-age marriages. But the government rejected the proposal, as did its successor, headed by Prime Minister Deve Gowda, in 1996.

"It has been the consistent policy of the government not to interfere in the personal laws of the distinct communities unless the initiative comes from the communities themselves," the government said in a statement. "The government is of the view that it is only through social and economic upliftment of these sections of the community that the practice can be eradicated."

CHILD MARRIAGE RESTRAINT ACT, 1929

(XIX OF 1929)

An Act to restraint the solemnization of child marriages.

Whereas it is expedient to restrain the solemnization of child marriages:

It is hereby enacted as follows:

1. Short titled, extent and commencement.

(1) This Act may be called the Child Marriage Restraint Act (1929).

(2) It extends to the whole of Pakistan and applies to all citizens of Pakistan wherever they may be.

(3) It shall come into force on the 1st day of April, 1939.

2. Definitions.

In this Act, unless there is anything repugnant in the subject or context,

(a) "child" means a person who, if a male, is under eighteen years of age, and if a female, is under sixteen years of age;

(b) "child marriage" means a marriage to which either of the contracting parties is a child;

(c) "contracting party" to a marriage means either of the parties whose marriage is or is about to be thereby solemnized;

(d) "minor" means person of either sex who is under eighteen years of age,

(e) "Union Council" means the Union Council or the Town Committee constituted under the Law relating to Local Government for the time being in force.

PUNJAB AMENDMENT IN SECTION 2:

(i) at the end of clause ©, the word "and" shall be added;

(ii) the comma appearing at the end of clause (d) shall be replaced by a full stop; and

(iii) clause e shall be omitted.

Punjab Ordinance, 23 of 1971.

3. Omitted by Muslim Family Laws Ordinance, 1961 (VIII of 1961 S. 12 (w.e.f. 15.07.1961).

4. Punishment for male adult above eighteen years of age marrying a child.

Whoever, being a male above eighteen years of age, contracts child marriage shall be punishable with simple imprisonment which may extend to one month, or with fine which may extend to one thousand rupees, or with both.

5. Punishment for solemnizing a child marriage.

Whoever performs, conducts or directs any child marriage shall be punishable with simple imprisonment which may extend to one month, or with fine which may extend to one thousand rupees, or with both, unless he proves that he had reason to believe that the marriage was not a child marriage.

6. Punishment for parent or guardian concerned in a child marriage.

(1) Where a minor contracts a child marriage any person having charge of the minor, whether as parent or guardian or in any other capacity, lawful or unlawful, who does any act to promote the marriage or permits it to be solemnized, or negligently fails to prevent it from being solemnized, shall be punishable with simple imprisonment which may extend to one month, or with fine which may extend to one thousand rupees, or with both: Provided that no woman shall be punishable with imprisonment.

(2) For the purpose of this section, it shall be presumed, unless and until the contrary is proved, that where a minor has contracted a child marriage, the person having charge of such minor has negligently failed to prevent the marriage from being solemnized.

7. Imprisonment not to be awarded for offence under section 3.

Notwithstanding anything contained in section 25 of the General Clauses At, 1897, or section 64 of the Pakistan

Penal Code, Court sentencing an offender under section 3 shall not be competent to direct that, in default of payment of-the fine imposed, he shall undergo only term of imprisonment.

8. Jurisdiction under this Act.

Notwithstanding anything contained in section 90 of the Code of Criminal Procedure, 1898, no Court other than that of a Magistrate of the First Class shall take cognizance of or try any offence under this Act.

9. Mode of taking cognizance of offence.

No Court shall take cognizance of any offence under this Act except on a complaint made by the Union Council, or if there is no Union Council in the area, by such authority as the Provincial Government may in this behalf prescribe, and such cognizance shall in no case be taken after the expiry of one year from the date on which the offence is alleged to have been committed.

PUNJAB AMENDMENT

In section 9:

The words and commas "except on a complaint made by the Union Council, or if there is no Union Council in the area, by such authority as the Provincial Government may in this behalf prescribe, and such cognizance shall in no case be taken" occurring after the words "under this Act" and before the words "after the expiry" shall be omitted.

Punjab Ordinance, 23 of 1971, S. 3.

10. Preliminary inquiries into offences under this Act.

The Court taking cognizance of an offence under this Act shall, unless it dismisses the complaint under section 203 of the Code of Criminal Procedure, 1898, either itself make an inquiry under section 202 of that Code or direct a Magistrate of the First Class subordinate to it to make such inquiry.

11. Omitted by Muslim Family Laws Ordinance, 1961.

12. Power to issue injunction prohibiting marriage in contravention of this Act.

(1) Notwithstanding anything to the contrary contained in this Act, the Court may, if satisfied from information laid before it through a complaint or otherwise that a child marriage in contravention of this Act has been arranged or is about to be solemnized, issue an injunction against any of the persons mentioned in sections 3, 4, 5 and 9 of this Act prohibiting such marriage.

(2) No injunction under sub-section (1) shall be issued against any person unless the Court has previously given notice to such person, and has afforded him an opportunity to show-cause against the issue of the injunction.

(3) The Court may either on its own motion or on the application of any person aggrieved, rescind or alter any order made under sub-section (1).

(4) Where such an application is received, the Court shall afford the applicant an early opportunity of appearing before it either in person or by pleader, and if the Court rejects the application wholly or in part, it shall record in writing its reasons for so doing.

(5) Whoever, knowing that an injunction has been issued against him under sub-section (1) of this section disobeys such injunction shall be punished with imprisonment of either description for a term which may extend to three months, or with fine which may extend to one thousand rupees, or with both: Provided that no woman shall be punishable with imprisonment.

CHILD BRIDES OF INDIA

"I am one of those unfortunate Hindu women whose hard lot is to suffer the unnameable miseries entailed by the custom of early marriage. This wicked practice of child marriage has destroyed the happiness of my life. It comes between me and the things which I prize above all others-study and mental cultivation. Without the least fault of mine I am doomed to seclusion; every aspiration of mine to rise above my ignorant sisters is looked down upon with suspicion and is interpreted in the most uncharitable manner."

-Extract from a letter written by Rukhmabai, a victim of child marriage, to The Times of India on June 26, 1885, and reproduced in the book Child Marriages in India by Jaya Sagade (Oxford University Press, 2005).

ONE hundred and twenty years later, India is still unable to stop this feudal practice. This is evident from the recent attack on an anganwadi (welfare centre) supervisor in Madhya Pradesh who tried to prevent three young girls from being married off in a mass ceremony.

Shakuntala Verma, the official, went to Bhangarh village in Dhar district on May 11 after a tip-off that a family there was planning to marry off its young daughters. As instructed by the Sub Divisional Magistrate she asked for proof of the girls' ages, but was forced to leave after members of the family threatened her. Later that evening a person armed with a sword came to her house and began slashing at her. As she tried to protect herself, one hand was severed and the other severely cut. Even as Shakuntala was fighting for her life in an Indore hospital after a nine-hour operation to re-attach her hand, Madhya Pradesh Chief Minister Babulal Gaur announced that "no serious action" would be taken against those who conduct child marriages. "Social customs are stronger than laws," he said.

The shocking incident renewed the debate on child marriage, which, though outlawed, is continuing openly in places such as Dhar- district and Krishnagiri district in Tamil Nadu. Most child marriages in northern India take place on an auspicious day-Akha Teej (Akshaya Trithiya). But in the south there appears to be no special occasion for such marriages.

Although the illegality of the practice and the fact that such marriages are not registered make the exact numbers hard to determine, some estimates put the number of child marriages in the country at several thousands every year. In some cases, the bride and the groom are said to be little more than toddlers, though the majority are in their teens.

There is considerable evidence that child marriages contribute to virtually every social problem that affects women.

According to Jaya Sagade, who has done extensive research on child marriages in India, marriages in the Vedic period were performed when the couples reached a mature age. The girl's consent was always sought. She even had the freedom to choose her life partner. This practice, says Jaya Sagade, continued until the sixth and seventh centuries. But there appears to have been a reversal thereafter. The patriarchal social structure that emerged seems to have given its sanction to the practice of child marriage, if one goes by the fact that ancient scriptures and customs suggest early marriage for the girl-preferably before puberty and certainly immediately after her first menstruation. According to some sociologists, the ancient erotic text the Kama Sutra talks indirectly of this practice when it warns that a girl who has "fully arrived at puberty" should be avoided as a wife.

Some people also trace the practice back to foreign invasions that began more than 1,000 years ago. The invaders were said to have carried away young girls as war booty, forcing local communities to marry off their daughters very young. To protect the women from sexual exploitation and to preserve their chastity, pre-puberty marriages began to be considered the best option. Over time, this became a custom, the violation of which was met with social disapproval and disgrace. It was even considered a sin to keep a girl in her parental home after she had attained puberty.

Among the other reasons cited for the continuance of the practice were: tradition, family and societal pressure, feudal set-up, and poverty. Based on the view that `virginity' is essential in a bride, girls are married off at a very young age, beginning five years. As a result, these girls are traumatised by sex and are forced to bear children much before their bodies are fully mature.

Many parents say they are scared to keep their daughters unmarried after puberty as they have a big responsibility of protecting them. Most parents cite poverty as the reason. They find it so difficult to feed everyone in the family that they prefer to "send off" the daughter as early as possible to some other family. As for the boy's family, it gets an "unpaid servant" to do the household chores, often along with dowry.

However, according to Rajeev Gupta, Professor of Sociology in Rajasthan University, the reasons for child marriage today go beyond custom and poverty. The oppressed classes and castes, with the encouragement of the landed castes, emulate this feudal social practice as it ensures for them a source of cheap family labour. He believes that it is in the interest of the dominant classes to keep this system going.

It is also the observation of the United Nations Children's Fund (UNICEF) that poor families may regard a young girl as an economic burden and her marriage as a necessary survival strategy for her family. UNICEF is of the opinion that there may be several reasons why parents get their daughters married off early.

They may think that early marriage offers protection from the dangers of sexual assault or more generally, offers the care of a male guardian. Early marriage may also be seen as a strategy to avoid girls becoming pregnant outside marriage. But there is no doubt that these notions get an impetus in an environment that basically goes against the girl child and women. There is no doubt that the affluent and the well off do not indulge in this practice, as the system is favourable to them in every sense.

Discussions on the evils of child marriage began as early as the last century. But a law-The Child Marriage Restraint Act (CMRA)-was introduced only in 1929. In fact, the Indian political class woke up to the reality when Census 1921 reported that there were 600 brides between the ages of one and 12 months.

It is said that a shocked Mahatma Gandhi urged a member of the Central Legislative Council, Harbilas Sarda, to introduce a Bill restraining child marriages. Thus was born the CMRA, popularly known as the Sarda Act. It was amended in 1978, when the minimum age of marriage was fixed at 21 for boys and 18 for girls and offences under the Act were made cognisable. The provisions of the Act are only to restrain and not to invalidate such marriages (see separate story on legal issues).

Several decades later, child marriages still take place with brazen impunity. The Central government does not have any records of child marriages; the argument is that the CMRA is administered and implemented by State governments and Union Territories. Therefore, the only institutions that do such tabulation are the Census of India and the National Family Health Survey (NFHS). According to Census 1991, the percentage of married females in the total number of females in the age group 10 to 14 was-13.2 in Rajasthan, the highest in the country. In second place was Madhya Pradesh at 8.5 per cent, followed by Uttar Pradesh at 7.1. For the country, the percentage of married women under the age of 18 stood at 53.3. The situation did not change substantially in the following decade. Census 2001 reports that there are nearly three lakh girls under 15 who have given birth to at least one child.

Villages such as Kottaiyur Kollai, an interior hamlet in the Aiyyur forest range in Krishnagiri district, contribute substantially to this number. An economically and socially backward village, it is inhabited by Poojari Irula tribal people, who were shifted to government-built group houses there from the remote forest caves in 2003. Most middle-aged women here said they were married off when they were four or five years old. Their marriage with a relative was usually decided as soon as they were born. According to the women, "the age of marriage for girls has now risen to eight".

Many women in this village have delivered 10 to 12 children. M. Muthamma is just 20 and has five surviving children. She was married at 10. Mallamma Malli is only a year older to Muthamma and has eight children, having married at the age of eight. Mallamma is also 20 and has six children; she was married at 12. Most of the children go to a school, run by Myrada, a non-governmental organisation (NGO), mainly because they get at least one meal a day. Bethamugilalam panchayat, which comes under the Kelamangalam Panchayat Union in Krishnagiri district, has a school with 300 children and two teachers, said S. Chennappan, the Panchayat Union president. The teachers come from Denganikottai, 25 km away, by the 11 a.m. bus and return by the 2 p.m. bus. After taking into account the lunch break, they teach hardly for an hour. Said Chennapan: "Poor transportation is an important reason for poor education in-several interior villages."

The women are keen that their children study and live better lives than theirs. But they are not sure how many generations it will take for their dream to come true. No one can be sure how long it will take, given the conditions prevailing in these villages. They have no infrastructure such as roads, hospitals and schools worth the name and some of the villages are not even accessible. According to Muthamma, the nearest hospital from Kottaiyur Kollai is in Denganikottai. The hospital, according to V. Nagarathinam of the All India Democratic Women's Association (AIDWA), has had no gynaecologist for several months; only recently was a woman doctor appointed after protests by AIDWA. According to Mallamma Malli, nearly 99 per cent of the deliveries happen at home and the rest, which are complicated, mostly end in the death of the woman.

Thirtham village under Veepanapalli Panchayat Union in the district is home to about 30 families, most of whose breadwinners are petty traders. Each family, on an average, has five surviving children. Everyone is surprised that child marriage, the norm in the village, should be an issue at all. Rani (12) of the village was married to Shankar (14) on February 3, just 10 days after she attained puberty. Shankar's mother K. Rathnamma alleged that after media reports on the marriage, the district administration and the police harassed them and Rani's family. As a result, they sent away Rani to her parents, who refused to take her in. Rani was literally on the street, ostracised by the entire village, when G. Geetha of the Village Reconstruction and Development Project (VRDP), an NGO, took her under the organisation's care and later, with the consent of Rani's family and the police, admitted her in a children's home in Omalur. Shankar continues to live in the village and he told

Frontline that he may consider another marriage if Rani does not return.

Whether she does or not, the Ranis of Krishnagiri and elsewhere have no say in the decision, victims as they are of an abominable practice that takes away from children their childhood in the quest of a life that virtually has no future.

Child marriage usually refers to two separate social phenomena which are practiced in some societies. The first and more widespread practice is that of marrying a young child (generally defined as below the age of fifteen) to an adult. In practice this is almost always a young girl being married to a man.

The second practice is a form of arranged marriage in which the parents of two children from different families arrange a future marriage. In this practice, the individuals who become betrothed often do not meet one another until the wedding ceremony, which occurs when they are both of a marriageable age. Which age this is differs by local custom. In most practicing cultures, this age is at or after the onset of puberty.

Child marriage is prevalent in many cultures throughout human history, but has gradually diminished since some countries started to urbanize, changing the ways of life for the people of these countries. An increase in the advocation of human rights, whether as women's rights or as children's rights, has caused the traditions of child marriage to decrease greatly as it was considered unfair and dangerous for the children. Today, child marriage is usually only practiced in third world countries, where cultural practices and traditions remain and have a strong impact on the people, and where the living standards and conditions still create a strong incentive for child marriage. For example, it is still common in rural parts of Pakistan.

CHILD MARRIAGES MAY HAVE MANY PURPOSES

The nobility of some cultures tend to use child marriage among different factions or states as a method to secure political ties between them. For example, the son or daughter of the royal family of a weaker power would sometimes be arranged to marry into the royal family of a stronger neighbouring power, thus preventing itself from being assimilated. In the lower classes, if they were fortunate, families could use child marriages as means to gain financial ties with wealthier people, ensuring their successions.

In child betrothals, a child's parents arrange a match with the parents of a child from another family (social standing, wealth and expected education all play a part), thus unilaterally determining the child's future at a young age. It is thought by adherents that physical attraction is not a suitable foundation upon which to build a marriage and a family. A separate consideration is the age at which the wedding, as opposed to the engagement, takes place.

Families are able to cement political and/or financial ties by having their children inter-marry. The betrothal is considered a binding contract upon the families and the children. The breaking of a betrothal can have serious consequences both for the families and for the betroven individuals themselves.

Africa

Despite many countries enacting a marriageable age of 16-18, customary marriages are widespread. Poverty, tradition and conflict make the incidence of child marriage in Sub-Saharan Africa similar to South Asia.

In many tribal systems a man pays a dowry to the girl's family in order to marry. This in many parts of Africa decreases as a girl gets older. Even before puberty it is common for a married girl to leave her parents to be with her 'husband'. Many of the marriages therefore are poverty related, with parents seeking a dowry to feed, clothe, educate and house the rest of the family. A male child in these countries is still more likely to gain a full education, gain employment/pursue a working life and therefore they tend to marry later. In Mali the girl:boy ratio of marriage before age 18 is 72:1; in Kenya, 21:1.

The various UN commissioned reports indicate that in many Sub-Saharan countries there is a high incidence of marriage among girls aged less than 15. Many governments have tended to overlook the particular problems which child marriage has resulted in, including obstetric fistulae, prematurity, childbirth mortality, sexually transmitted diseases, including cervical cancer, and malaria. In parts of Ethiopia and Nigeria over 50% of girls are married before the age of 15. In parts of Mali 39% of girls are married before the age of 15. In Niger and Chad over 70% of girls are married before the age of 18. In South Africa there are legal provisions made for respecting the marriage laws of traditional marriages, whereby a person might be married as young as 12 for females and 14 for males.

United States

While child marriage is illegal in the United States, at least one religious group-the Fundamentalist Church of Jesus Christ of Latter Day Saints, has allegedly practiced child marriage as part of its polygamy. Church leader Warren Jeffs was convicted of being an accomplice to rape of a minor due to this practice.

South Asia

India

Child marriage has been illegal in India since the passing of the Child Marriage Restraint Act, 1929. In this Act, the term child refers to a male younger than twenty-one, or a female younger than eighteen. A marriage falls under the scope of this Act if either of the contracting parties meets its definition of child. Every year children are still married illegally in India. Most of the child marriages in India take place in rural villages and areas, that usually have little legal supervision. Over time, child marriage has become a social taboo, with the majority of Indians believing it to be wrong. However, this still occurs. According to "National Plan of Action for Children 2005", (Published by Department of Women and Child Development of India) a goal has been setup to eliminate child marriage completely by 2010. This plan has proved to be successful, but it is still very difficult to monitor all children due to the sheer size of the Indian Subcontinent.

Pakistan

Child marriage has been restrained in Pakistan through the Child Marriage Restraint Act, 1929. But still widely practiced in some areas through Vani and other ceremonies.

Bangladesh

Over 40% of girls are married before reaching 15 years of age (approximately 45% according to the majority of recent surveys) in Bangladesh. The Ministry of Women and Children Affairs is making progress in increasing women's education and employment opportunities. This, combined with specific education about child marriage and cooperation with religious leaders should help to decrease child marriage.

South East Asia

Child Marriage Prevention Programs

The programs are organized as follows:

Implementing Organization, Program Name, Location; (Time Frame).

Brief Description

Source

Asia

Indian Institute of Young Inspirers, A Communication Strategy for the Promotion of Adolescent Reproductive Health, Lucknow, Uttar Pradesh, India; (2003-2005).

This program developed innovative communication strategies for adolescents with an emphasis on sexuality, gender, violence and early marriage.

Mamta Health Institute for Mother and Child, Action Approach for Reduction of Early Marriage and Early Pregnancy in the State of Rajasthan, Rajasthan, India; (2002-2005).

This program sought to delay age at marriage and create an environment supportive of delayed first pregnancy through providing training on early marriage and early pregnancy (EMEP). It also created a newsletter for young people focusing on EMEP.

BRAC, Adolescent Development Programme (ADP), Bangladesh; (2000-ongoing).

The ADP seeks to improve the quality of life of vulnerable adolescents, and to reduce child marriage through addressing child rights sensitization, child marriage, HIV/AIDS, involvement of parents and the community in girls' participation in society, and other issues via life skills activities, non-formal education, community sensitization and income generation.

BRAC, Adolescent Reproductive Health Education (ARHE) Program, Bangladesh; (1995-ongoing).

The ARHE creates a curriculum for boys and girls age 12 and older with no education that includes physical and mental changes during adolescence, pregnancy, guidance about age at marriage, STIs, gender issues, male and female roles in reproduction, and violence against women and girls.

National Commission for Women, Amendments to Child Marriage Restraint Act, India; (1992-ongoing).

The National Commission for Women proposed amendments to the India's Child Marriage Restraint Act including more stringent penalties for offenders and compulsory registration of all marriages. They organized anti-child marriage agitation in four states-Rajasthan, Uttar Pradesh, Madhya Pradesh and Andhra Pradesh.

Haryana Government, Apni Beti, Apna Dhan (My Daughter, My Pride), India; (1994-ongoing).

The ABAD scheme entitles the mother of a newly-born girl-child to Rs. 500 and Rs. 2,500 per year, cashable only after the child is 18 years old. This program helps reduce infanticide and improve the status of girl children.

The Government of Nepal, UNFPA, Arrange the Marriage of Your Daughter After 20 Years of Age poster, Nepal, (1995).

The government of Nepal created materials encouraging parents to delay marriage of their daughters, including posters educating adults about the negative consequences of early marriage.

Plan International-Nepal, Basic Life Options, Nepal.

The program educates adolescents about sexual health, reproduction, legal rights and risks such as early marriage and sexual exploitation. There are campaigns to register births to protect children against early marriage in the future.

UNICEF, Pakistan Boy Scouts Association, Brothers Join Meena, Pakistan, Pakistan.

Through this program, each boy collects data from 10 neighboring households on health, sanitation and educational status. In return, the program provides information on various issues, including the importance of education for girls. They then monitor the progress of each household. The program empowers adolescent boys to promote and protect children's rights, including the girl's right to education-a key defense against early marriage.

International Center for Research on Women (ICRW), Development Initiative on Supporting Healthy Adolescents (DISHA), Bihar and Jharkhand, India; (2003-2005)

This program helps increase access to family planning and reproductive health services for married and unmarried youth, delay marriage and childbearing, provide youth with alternatives to early marriage through enhanced livelihoods skills and options, and build the capacity of local NGOs to promote the reproductive health of young people.

Bangladesh Women's Health Coalition, Academy for Educational Development (AED), John Snow International (JSI), Empowerment of Women Research Program, Bangladesh; (2003 to 2005).

This program focuses on empowering women and address topics such as delayed age at marriage, postponement of childbearing and improved economic opportunities. They use research on factors influencing decisions on timing of marriage and childbearing to develop national and local interventions.

The Tata Iron and Steel Company (TISCO), Family Welfare Programme, India; (1993).

TISCO sought to establish a model of corporate action to help young people become informed on sexual and reproductive health matters in order to prevent child marriage, premarital sex and deaths of young mothers. Income was generated for the project through performances of the CFI Drama Troupe consisting of unemployed young people.

Population Council, Child In Need Institute-Kolkata, Deepak Charitable Trust-Vadodara, International Institute for Population Sciences-Mumbai, First time Parents Project, India; (2003-2005).

The project organized activities providing reproductive health information to married girls, their partners and influential adults and empowering young, married women through group formation. Child Survival India, Gender Sensitization Programme, India.

A gender sensitization program in schools and the community that promotes community discussions and debates on gender inequalities, including early marriage, in order to find effective solutions.

PCI, Hum Raahi (Come Along With Me) soap opera, India; (1991-1994).

A television serial promoted women's equality and development, encouraging education, delayed marriage, the equal value of girl children and other health issues to an estimated 100 million viewers.

Government of Indonesia, Indonesia's National Marriage Act, Indonesia; (1974).

Indonesia's National Marriage Act made marriage registration in parts of the country dependent on evidence that the marriage is neither forced nor polygamous and on attendance at an educational session on reproduction.

Food and Agriculture Organization of the United Nations (FAO), Department of Foreign Technical and Economic Cooperation of Dingxi Prefecture, Culture Department of Dingxi Prefecture, Integration Population Education Programs of Rural Youth in China, China; (1994-1995).

Pilot school projects reported that following exposure to population education, students who had agreed to postpone marriage were sticking to their agreement.

Institute for Health Management, Pachod (IHMP), International Center for Research on Women (ICRW), Life Skills Intervention on Age at Marriage in Maharashtra, Rural Maharashtra, India; (1999-present).

The program led community-based life skills intervention to delay marriage, improve health and social status, promote self development and increase girls' self-confidence.

Myrada, Plan International, Madakasira Project, India; (unknown-2009).

Organized children's groups in one community to address child marriage and bonded labor.

International Center for Research on Women (ICRW), EngenderHealth, New ERA Ltd., BP Memorial Health Foundation, Nepal Adolescent Project (NAP), Nepal; (1998 to 2003).

An "Information, Education and Communication" (IEC) program included discussions on reproductive health topics for youth and community fairs to provide information to young people to increase adolescents' knowledge of reproductive health and to change social norms around early marriage and childbearing.

Pathfinder International, PRACHAR Project: Promoting Change in the Reproductive Behavior of Youth, Bihar, India; (2001-2005). The program conducted trainings and community meetings to teach adolescents about STIs, HIV/AIDS, and delaying and spacing children with the plan of improving reproductive health and changing traditional customs of early marriage. The program teaches families and respected elders/leaders about benefits of delaying and spacing children.

The Human Rights Law Network (HRLN) of the Socio Legal Information Centre (SLIC), MacArthur Foundation, Reproductive and Sexual Rights of Young People in India, India; (2003-ongoing).

This is a program of education and dissemination of information on gender-just laws and the promotion of judicial recognition of reproductive health as a part of the fundamental right to health, in support of legal initiative to discourage early marriage in India.

Government of Sri Lanka, Sri Lanka Child Marriage Legislation, Sri Lanka; (1995)

Legislation was passed that was successful in raising marriage age by driving legislative reforms requiring that all marriages be registered and that consent of both marriage partners be recorded. Specific cases of non-consensual marriages arranged by parents was deemed invalid.

Government of Bangladesh, World Bank, The Female Secondary School Assistance Project (FSSAP), Bangladesh; (1993-ongoing).

This program seeks to increase enrollment of girls in secondary school and delay marriage by addressing financial and other constraints for attending school. Parents are required to sign a bond that daughters will not marry before age 18.

UNICEF, BRAC, the Centre for Mass Education in Science (CMES), The Kishori Abhijan project, Bangladesh; (2001-2004).

This program provided girls with livelihood and leadership skills, peer education sessions on early marriage and reproductive health. Communities, parents and adolescent boys were sensitized to girls' needs and rights. The program also sponsored nation-wide advocacy campaigns.

Sajeda Amin, Ian Diamond, Ruchira T. Naved, and Margaret Newby, Transition to Adulthood of Female Garment-factory Workers in Bangladesh, Bangladesh; (1998).

This project conducted research to determine the effect of working in garment industry on female workers, including effect on age of marriage.

Government of Uttar Pradesh, UP Population Policy 2000, India; (2000-2016).

This program increases awareness about legal age at marriage using electronic media for dissemination. It seeks to ensure that panchayats maintain records of all marriages in their jurisdiction. It uses women's groups and religious and community leaders to change values and attitudes about child marriage.

Africa

CARE International-Eritrea, Haben, A Community-based Prevention and Response Program for Gender-based Violence, Gash Barka Zone of Eritrea; (2001-2004).

Local clinics established support groups for women to address gender equity, domestic violence, and Female Genital Cutting. Public awareness programs incorporated community-based and mass media awareness-raising activities. Early marriage was not originally an objective, but was raised as a concern by community members and was later incorporated into programming objectives.

Population Council, Adolescent Health and Information Projects, Federation of Muslim Women Associations of Nigeria, Addressing Child Marriage in Northern Nigeria, Nigeria; (2005-2009).

Collaborating with religious, female and community leaders, the intervention raises awareness and promotes dialogue on child marriage through existing community forums and radio spots.

World Learning for International Development, Basic Education Strategic Objective (BESO II) Community-

Government Partnership Program (CGPP), Ethiopia; (2002-ongoing).

The program seeks to promote gender equity, including ongoing campaigns against early marriage and female circumcision. It promotes the value of education for girls and involves men in advocating for delaying age at marriage.

Population Council, Ethiopian Ministry of Youth and Sports, Berhane Hewan, Amhara region, Ethiopia; 2004-2008.

The program promotes functional literacy, life skills and reproductive health education. Economic incentives (receiving a goat) encourage families to allow their daughters to participate in girls' groups and to remain in school.

Christian Children's Fund (CCF), Christian Children's Fund of Ethiopia program, Ethiopia; (ongoing).

The program raises community awareness around the physical dangers of child marriage.

Christian Children's Fund (CCF), Christian Children's Fund of Uganda program, Uganda; (ongoing).

Working with communities to combat the practice of forcing girls into marriage with men who have raped them due to the belief that they are "spoiled."

Christian Children's Fund (CCF), Christian Children's Fund of Zambia program, Zambia; (ongoing).

Focus on bringing girls back to school, promoting reproductive health education in schools and delaying marriage.

World Learning for International Development (WLID), USAID, Community Action for Girls' Education (CAGE), Benin; (2001-2004).

This program rescued trafficked girls and girls in danger of early marriages. It advocated for girls' schooling and enabled family and community dialogues on gender equality and early marriage.

The Association for the Protection of the Environment (APE), Egypt's Maqattam garbage settlement, Egypt; (1995).

The program taught girls rug-making, paper recycling, and embroidery projects. A sum of E£500 (US$148) was offered to any girl who deferred her marriage until age 18, and who entered marriage of her own free will.

Johns Hopkins Bloomberg School of Public Health's Center for Communication Programs/Health Communication Partnership-Egypt Field Office, The Academy for Educational Development (AED), Family Planning Project-Egypt, Egypt; (1988-1993).

The program was a mass multimedia program that targeted young married women to address family planning issues. It focused on increasing communication between spouses, promoting male responsibility and reducing early marriage. It used 17-50 minute TV or radio drama episodes, contests, music videos and soap operas.

Population Council, PATH Kenya, Kendu Adventist Hospital, Highlighting Marital Risk and Promoting Premarital Voluntary Counseling and Testing in Nyanza, Kenya; (2005-2008).

This project is a large-scale educational campaign on dangers of early marriage and promoting Voluntary Counseling and Testing (VCT) for HIV among newly married couples and those considering marriage. It uses community theater, radio broadcasts and religious leaders to raise awareness. The project demonstrated local demand for increasing age of marriage by building on a meeting of religious leaders.

CARE International UK, Integrated Women's Health and Empowerment Program (IWEP), Gash Barka Zone of Eritrea; (2006-2008).

The project is designed to strengthen coping mechanisms of women-headed households in poor, conflict-affected communities in Eritrea. It raises awareness about reproductive and sexual health, HIV/AIDS, female genital mutilation and early marriage. It aims to strengthen relevant national support structures and existing services.

Save the Children Egypt, Population Council, ISHRAQ project, Egypt; (2001-2004).

This program worked to improve life opportunities for rural out-of-school girls, ages 13-15, by improving literacy, recreational opportunities, livelihood skills, health practices and mobility; positively influencing social norms about girls; improving local and national support for girl-friendly policies; and developing positive attitudes of communities and families toward educating girls. The efforts reduced acceptance of early marriage.

Moroccan government, King of Morocco Calls for Fundamental Reform in Family Law, Morocco; (2003).

Morocco's new family code raised the minimum age of marriage for girls, making it the same age as for boys. The government also organized a large-scale media campaign to raise awareness of the new law and encourage behavior change. Christian Children's Fund (CCF), Naningoi Girls' Boarding School, Kenya; (1999-ongoing). This program seeks to rescue underage Maasai girls from early marriage and enroll them in formal studies instead.

The Centre for Development and Population Activities (CEDPA), New Horizons Program, Egypt; (1994-2004).

This was a non-formal education program for girls. Girls were given 100 sessions of life skills training and reproductive health knowledge, including the issue of marriage. It was implemented through 365 NGOs and youth centers. Family Health Options Kenya (formerly Family Planning Association of Kenya), Plan International Kenya,

Programme for Appropriate Technology in Health (PATH), Kenyan Ministry of Education and Health, Options Project for Improving the Status of Women, Kenya.

This program identifies girls married at an early age and lobbies to have marriages dissolved; and provides shelter and education for girls released from forced marriage. It raises community awareness through information, education and communication (IEC) materials.

Forum on Marriage and the Rights of Women and Girls, Ouagadougou Declaration on Early and Forced Marriage, Burkina Faso, Ghana, The Gambia, Mali, Nigeria and Sudan; (2003).

This declaration calls upon governments to end child marriage. The Futures Group, USAID, POLICY Project, Malawi; (2002-2004).

This project reviewed all HIV-related laws and policies, and proposed amendments. It lobbied with the law commission and parliament to change the legal age of marriage to16.

Nike Foundation; Population Council; United Nations Foundation; United Nations Population Foundation (UNFPA); and the Ethiopian Ministry of Youth, Sports and Culture, Preventing Early Marriage in Ethiopia, Ethiopia.

In rural areas, girls receive non-formal education and health information and services. Open dialogue encourages community members to expand traditional options for girls, including delaying marriage. In urban slums, the program aims to promote safety and social support for girls.

Tostan, Senegal, Program on the Abandonment of FGC and Early Marriage, Senegal; (1982-ongoing).

A holistic basic education program where over 12,000 villagers attended regular classes on democracy, human rights, problem-solving, hygiene and health. Training in implementing practical development activities follows, involving all community members and leading to declarations against female genital cutting (FGC) and early marriage.

Coalition of Nigerian NGOs, Role of NGOs in Implementing the Beijing Platform for Action (BPFA), Nigeria; (1995-2005).

The NGOs pushed for legislation (Child Rights Bill) to outlaw marriage before the age of 18 and to ensure that girls who have babies during their school years continue their education.

Creative Centre for Community Mobilisation (CRECCOM), USAID, Social Mobilization Campaign for Educational Quality (SMC-EQ), Malawi; (1998-2004).

The program used a social mobilization approach to mobilize individuals and communities to support education, particularly for girls. It also included a message about delaying marriage. Pugsada, Support Centres for Girl Brides in Burkina Faso, Burkina Faso; (1998).

Puksata, a local NGO, works with three Catholic religious centers that shelter girls who have run away from forced or early marriage. Puksata works with the centers to provide the girls with vocational training and mediates between the families and the girls.

Population Council, K-Rep Development Agency (KDA), Tap and Reposition Youth (TRY), Kenya; (1998-2005).

The project hopes to ascertain whether the experience of running a business can alter a girl's self-image and her relationships with others. Reproductive health training is included as a component of the project.

World Vision Ethiopia, The Adjibar Safe Motherhood Project, Ethiopia.

The project works in collaboration with the local government, schools, community and influential religious leaders on all aspects of safe motherhood, including: education on the harms of early marriage, family planning, HIV/AIDS education, and pre and post-natal care.

Oxfam Great Britain, government of Kenya, The Mobile School Project, Kenya.

This is a non-formal education program for girls not attending school that led to a fall in early marriage and helped women assert themselves. Communication for Change (C4C), American Refugee Committee (ARC), Through Our Eyes Project, Guinea and Liberia; (2006).

In this community media project, audiences watch videos, discuss themes raised in them and share personal stories. One video covers forced marriage.

Pathfinder International, Women's and Girl's Empowerment Project, Ethiopia.

Working with religious leaders, and organizational partners, such as the Ethiopian Women's Lawyers Association to address AIDS and change cultural practices, including early marriage.

Plan International, Malawi.

Community sensitization and training on children's rights, and developed a district-level child protection policy. They also assisted in lobbying for bills on increasing the age of marriage and birth registration.

Plan International-Niger, Niger.

This project works with village leaders to reinforce importance of girls' education and school youth programs. On the national level, it works with Ministry of Social Affairs to implement the Code for the Child to discourage early marriage.

The Addis Ababa Fistula Hospital, the Ethiopian Women Lawyers Association (EWLA), Ethiopia. The hospital has a joint program with EWLA to advise patients of their rights. Hospital outreach centers alert women's groups in the provinces to the dangers of early marriage and childbirth. EWLA campaigns for observance of the legal marriage age.

Latin America

Population Council, Creating Opportunities for Mayan Adolescent Girls, Guatemala; (2004-ongoing).

This project supports schooling for girls and increasing livelihood skills. Girls meet weekly for life skills, financial literacy, functional literacy, sports and possibly microfinance activities, all aimed at delaying marriage.

Cross-Regional

UNICEF, Meena Initiative (South Asia) and the Sara Adolescent Girl Communication Initiative (East and Southern Africa), South Asia, Eastern Africa and Southern Africa; (1995-1999). The young cartoon heroine of a multimedia package is a catalyst for discussion on the importance of staying in school, HIV/AIDS, domestic workload, FGM/FGC and early marriage.

UNFPA, UNIFEM, UNICEF, the Population Council, International Planned Parenthood Federation, Bangladesh, Ethiopia and India.

This is a special project to improve social and economic opportunities for adolescent girls by producing evidence-based strategies to find feasible alternatives to child marriage. It includes mobilization of community and opinion leaders.

2

CHILD MARRIAGE RESTRAINT ACT, 1929

SHORT TITLE, EXTENT AND COMMENCEMENT

(1) This Act may be called the Child Marriage Restraint Act, 2[1929].

3[(2) It extends to the whole of India 4[except the State of Jammu and Kashmir]; and it applies also to all citizens of India without and beyond India].5

(3) It shall come into force on the 1st day of April, 1930.

DEFINITIONS

In this Act, unless there is anything repugnant in the subject or context,-

[(a) "child" means a person who, if a male, has not completed twenty-one years of age, and if a female, has not completed eighteen years of age;]

(b) "child marriage" means a marriage to which either of the contracting parties is a child;

(c) "contracting party" to a marriage means either of the parties whose marriage is 7[or is about to be] thereby solemnized; and

(d) "minor" means a person of either sex who is under eighteen years of age.

PUNISHMENT FOR MALE ADULT BELOW TWENTY-ONE YEARS OF AGE MARRYING A CHILD

Whoever, being a male above eighteen yēars of age and below twenty-one, contracts a child marriage [shall be punishable with simple imprisonment which may extend to fifteen days, or with fine which may extend to one thousand rupees, or with both].

Punishment for Male Adult above Twenty-one Years of Age Marrying a Child

Whoever, being a male above twenty-one years of age, contracts a child marriage shall be punishable with 9[simple imprisonment which may extend to three months and shall also be liable to fine].

Punishment for Solemnizing a Child Marriage

Whoever performs, conducts or directs any child marriage shall be punishable with 9[simple imprisonment which may extend to three months and shall also be liable to fine], unless he proves that he had reason to believe that the marriage was not a child marriage

Punishment for Parent or Guardian Concerned in a Child Marriage

(1) Where a minor contracts a child marriage, any person having charge of the minor, whether as parent or guardian or in any other capacity, lawful or unlawful, who does any act to promote the marriage or permits it to be solemnized, or negligently fails to prevent it from being solemnized, shall be punishable with 9[simple imprisonment which may extend to three months and shall also be liable to fine]:Provided that no woman shall be punishable with imprisonment.

(2) For the purposes of this section, it shall be presumed, unless and until the contrary is proved, that where

a minor has contracted a child marriage, the person having charge of such minor has negligently failed to prevent the marriage from being solemnized.

Offences to be Cognizable for Certain Purposes

10[The Code of Criminal Procedure, 1973, shall apply to offences under this Act as if they were cognizable offences-

(a) for the purpose of investigation of such offences; and

(b) for the purposes of matters referred to in section 42 of that Code, and (ii) the arrest of a person without a warrant or without an order of a Magistrate.]

JURISDICTION UNDER THIS ACT

Notwithstanding anything contained in section 190 of the 11[Code of Criminal Procedure, 1973] no Court other than that of a 11[Metropolitan Magistrate or a Judicial Magistrate of the first class] shall take cognizance of, or try, any offence under this Act.

Mode of Taking Cognizance of Offences

No Court shall take cognizance of any offence under this Act after the expiry of one year from the date on which the offence is alleged to have been committed.]

Preliminary Inquiries into Offences

Any Court, on receipt of a complaint of an offence of which it is authorized to take cognizance, shall, unless it dismisses the complaint under section 203 of the 11[Code of Criminal Procedure, 1973], either itself make an inquiry under section 202 of that Code or direct a Magistrate subordinate to it to make such inquiry.]

Power to Take Security from Complainant-

Repealed by the Child Marriage Restraint (Amendment) Act, 1949]

Power to Issue Injunction Prohibiting Marriage in Contravention of this Act

(1) Notwithstanding anything to the contrary contained in this Act, the Court may, if satisfied from information laid before it through a complaint or otherwise that a child marriage in contravention of this Act has been arranged or is about to be solemnized, issue an injunction against any of the persons mentioned in sections 3, 4, 5 and 6 of this Act prohibiting such marriage.

(2) No injunction under sub-section (1) shall be issued against any person unless the Court has previously given notice to such person, and has afforded him an opportunity to show cause against the issue of the injunction.

(3) The Court may either on its own motion or on the application of any person aggrieved rescind or alter any order made under sub-section (1).

(4) Where such an application is received, the Court shall afford the applicant an early opportunity of appearing before it either in person or by pleader; and if the Court rejects the application wholly or in part, it shall record in writing its reasons for so doing.

(5) Whoever knowing that an injunction has been issued against him under sub-section (1) of this section disobeys such injunction shall be punished with imprisonment of either description for a term which may extend to three months, or with fine which may extend to one thousand rupees, or with both:

Provided that no woman shall be punishable with imprisonment.]

3

NEW INSIGHTS ON PREVENTING CHILD MARRIAGE

INTRODUCTION

One in seven girls in the developing world marries before 15 (Population Council 2006). Nearly half of the 331 million girls in developing countries are expected to marry by their 20th birthday. At this rate, 100 million more girls—or 25,000 more girls every day—will become child brides in the next decade (Bruce and Clark 2004).

The U.S. government and international community increasingly are concerned about the prevalence of child marriage and its toll on girls in developing countries (UNICEF 2005; Save the Children 2004; Mathur, Greene and Malhotra 2003). In response to congressional interest, the U.S. Agency for International Development (USAID) sought to learn more about the extent and effectiveness of current development efforts to reduce the prevalence of child marriage.

The Interagency Gender Working Group (IGWG) at USAID—a network of nongovernmental organizations and cooperating agencies working with USAID to promote gender equity in population, health and nutrition programs—found that although child marriage is closely related to other development efforts, the issue is not being addressed systematically within USAID programs. USAID country mission and cooperating agency staff could describe only a few activities that addressed child marriage either directly or indirectly in their programs. Furthermore, these activities are confined to only a few countries and implementing partners. Field staff also acknowledged that child marriage undermines other development efforts, and a number of staff provided thoughtful and strategic ideas for addressing child marriage through existing efforts.

IGWG commissioned this research to learn more about child marriage and programs working to curtail the practice.

Current literature on child marriage is focused primarily on examining the prevalence, consequences and reasons reported by parents for early marriage. Much less is known about the actual risk factors for child marriage, what may serve to protect girls from marrying too young, and how most effectively to change the social acceptance of early marriage. Identifying these factors would bolster efforts to design targeted interventions that prevent child marriage. A better understanding of risk and protective factors and social norms also could inform program designs to mitigate these risks and strengthen protective factors or create them where they do not exist.

The work presented here investigates two key questions:

- o What factors could be tracked and used to decrease risk of, or increase protection against, child marriage and ultimately could be targeted for prevention efforts?
- o What are the current programmatic approaches to prevent child marriage in developing countries, and are these programs effective? This report answers these questions in two ways: (1) by analyzing data

from Demographic and Health Surveys (DHS) to determine possible risk and protective factors for child marriage; and (2) by conducting a program scan to see how child marriage is addressed and to glean insights on program strengths.

The report is organized as follows. Section 2 provides a review of the literature on child marriage. Section 3 uses data from Demographic and Health Surveys (DHS) to determine countries with the highest prevalence of child marriage worldwide and to examine factors associated with early age at first marriage both at the country level and within the highest prevalence regions of these countries.

Section 4 offers insight into current programmatic approaches revealed through a Web-based program scan. Finally, Section 5 provides program and policy recommendations for preventing child marriage.

The authors believe the information in this report will be useful for policy-makers and development practitioners working on or planning a future program to prevent child marriage. New insights on risk and protective factors will help program designers find points of intervention, while the program scan offers a better understanding of what is being done on the ground. The authors hope that this work will lead to additional investments in innovative approaches to reduce child marriage.

REVIEW OF THE LITERATURE

The literature on child marriage has grown significantly in the last decade. Earlier research focused primarily on child marriage prevalence and consequences. Newer literature is beginning to explore factors that may help prevent child marriage, but is limited primarily to education and economic status and their known influences on child marriage. The research presented in this report examines these and other possible risk and protective factors for early marriage. Researchers for this report sought to include, but did not-find, literature summarizing or analyzing program experience to delay marriage.

Prevalence

According to Demographic and Health Surveys (DHS), which provide much of the current country-level child marriage data, child marriage is most common in the world's poorest countries.

The highest rates are in sub-Saharan Africa and South Asia as well as parts of Latin America and the Caribbean (ICRW 2006; NRC/IOM 2005). A UNICEF study found that 48 percent of women between 15 and 24 were married before 18 in South Asia. Prevalence is 42 percent in Africa (UNICEF 2005), and more than 60 percent in some parts of East and West Africa (IPPF and UNFPA 2006). In Latin America and the Caribbean, prevalence is 29 percent, though some individual countries have much higher rates (UNICEF 2005).

Child marriage also is common in the Middle East, where nearly half of girls younger than 18 in Yemen and Palestine are married (IPPF and UNFPA 2006).

The median age at marriage is rising around the world, including in developing countries (NRC/IOM 2005). In sub-Saharan Africa, for example, 21 of 30 countries have seen an increase in the national age at marriage over the past several decades (Westoff 2003). This trend is largely attributed to the increase of girls' educational attainment and the increased participation of women in the labor force (NRC/IOM 2005; Mathur, Greene and Malhotra 2003; United Nations 1987). This increase in the age at marriage is occurring slowly and unevenly within countries, however, and many girls are missed by this trend.

Negative Consequences

Child marriage not only is recognized as a human rights violation but also as a barrier to development. Considerable evidence shows that the negative consequences of child marriage are numerous and especially harmful for girls, their children and their communities. As described below, these consequences include poorer health outcomes for young mothers and their children as well as higher risk of HIV, and higher experiences of violence and abuse among girls married before age 18. Evidence also suggests early marriage results in lower levels of education and persistent poverty among girls.

Maternal Health

Studies show a strong association between child marriage and early childbirth, partly because girls are pressured to prove their fertility soon after marrying and they have little access to information on reproductive health or ability to influence decision making on family planning (Mathur, Greene and Malhotra 2003; Blesdoe and Cohen 1993; Mensch, Bruce and Greene 1998; Malhotra et al. 2003). Onethird of women in developing countries give birth before 20; in West Africa, as much as 55 percent of women give birth before 20 (Save the Children 2004).

Women who bear children at a young age may face serious health consequences. Young mothers experience higher rates of maternal mortality and higher risk of obstructed labor and pregnancy-induced hypertension because their bodies are unprepared for childbirth (Save the Children 2004; Mathur, Greene and Malhotra 2003). Girls between 10 and 14 are five times more likely than women ages 20 to 24 to die in pregnancy and childbirth (UNFPA and the University of Aberdeen 2004). Girls ages 15 to 19 are twice as likely as older women to die from childbirth and pregnancy, making pregnancy the leading cause of death in poor countries for this age group (Save the Children 2004). In Mali, for example, the maternal mortality ratio is 178 for every 100,000 live births of women ages 15 to 19, compared to only 32 for women ages 20 to 24 (FCI and the Safe Motherhood Inter-Agency Group 1998; CDC 2002).

Girls who have babies also have a high risk of suffering from obstetric fistula, a condition in which the vagina, bladder and/or rectum tear during childbirth and, if left untreated, causes lifelong leakage of urine and feces (UNFPA and EngenderHealth 2003). Two million women suffer from obstetric fistula worldwide, and an additional 50,000 to 100,000 new cases develop annually among girls (Murray and Lopez 1998).

Child marriage also exposes young married girls to a greater risk of HIV infection. A study in Kenya and Zambia found that 15-to 19-year-old married girls were 75 percent more likely to have HIV than sexually active, unmarried girls. Married girls may be more vulnerable to HIV infection because they have little option to change their sexual behavior even with knowledge about HIV (Clark 2004). Child brides also have less access to quality health care services and information compared to girls who marry when they are older (Mathur, Greene and Malhotra 2003; Mensch, Bruce and Green 1998; Singh and Samara 1996).

Infant Health

The children of teen mothers experience serious health consequences as well. A child born to a teen mother is twice as likely to die before the age of 1 as the child of a woman in her 20s. Currently, 1 million infants of young mothers die every year worldwide as a result of pregnancy and childbirth-related causes. If they survive, these infants tend to have higher rates of low birth weight, premature birth and infant mortality than those born to older mothers (Save the Children 2004). After birth, infants of teen mothers are more likely than infants born to older mothers to have poorer health care and inadequate nutrition as a result of their young mothers' poor feeding behavior (Save the Children 2004; Kurz 1997).

Education and Economic Status

Child marriage is associated with lower education and economic status of girls. Child brides are less able than older or unmarried girls to access schooling and income-generating opportunities or to benefit from education or economic development programs. Girls already in school are often forced to terminate their education when they marry early (Save the Children 2004). Limited mobility, household responsibilities, pregnancy and raising children, and other social restrictions for married girls prevent them from taking advantage of education or work opportunities (Mathur, Greene and Malhotra 2003).

Early childbearing and motherhood, which usually accompanies early marriage, also is associated with lower levels of education and higher rates of poverty (Singh and Samara 1996; Mensch, Bruce and Greene 1998). Opportunities for young mothers to continue their education or to work often are limited because they have little access to resources, and are responsible for childrearing and household tasks (Save the Children 2004). Thus, early childbearing, as well as early marriage, tends to preclude further education and reinforce poverty.

Domestic Violence and Decision Making

Girls who are married young often lack status and power within their marriages and households, and so are more likely to experience domestic violence, sexual abuse, and isolation from family and community (UNICEF 2005; Jenson and Thornton 2003). A survey in India found that girls who married before 18 reported experiencing physical violence twice as often as girls who married at a later age; younger married girls reported experiencing sexual violence three times more often (ICRW 2005). Girls who marry young are also more likely to believe violence is justified (UNICEF 2005; Jenson and Thornton 2003). A Kenya study found that 36 percent of girls who married before 18 believe that men are justified in beating their wives, compared to 20 percent of those who married at a later age (UNICEF 2005).

Lower status in the home also leaves married girls with less ability to influence decisions about their own lives (ICRW 2005; UNICEF 2005). Women who married as children are more likely to have partners who have the final say on household decisions, including their visits to family or friends, their health, their ability to work, large and small household purchases, and contraception (UNICEF 2005).

RISK AND PROTECTIVE FACTORS

The literature indicates that both income-earning activities and education protect girls by delaying marriage, especially of poor girls living in rural areas most at risk of child marriage (UNICEF 2005, Jenson and Thornton 2003). Evidence is scarce, however, on whether other factors are risks for or protect against child marriage.

Economic Status

The literature in this section shows that poverty increases risk for child marriage, and that income-generating activities for young women are protective. Research shows that the poorest countries have the highest child marriage rates. Child marriage is concentrated in the poorest countries, with the lowest gross domestic product countries tending to have the highest child marriage prevalence rates (ICRW 2006).

It is also most common among the poorest households. In a study of women ages 20 to 24 in 49 countries, child marriage was most common among the poorest 20 percent of households in every country. A girl from the poorest household in Senegal, for example, is more than four times as likely to marry before age 18 as a girl in the richest household (UNICEF 2005).

In Nigeria, 80 percent of the poorest girls marry before the age of 18, compared to 22 percent of the richest girls (UNFPA 2003).

Poverty leads to a higher prevalence of child marriage because poor families feel they have fewer resources and incentives to invest in alternative options for girls (Mathur, Greene and Malhotra 2003). Many families say they marry their daughters early because girls are an economic burden that can be relieved through marriage.

Additionally, in many countries, poor families reap economic benefits from dowry or bride wealth by marrying girls at younger ages (Berhane-Selaisse 1993; Tufts University Feinstein International Famine Center 2004; Mathur, Greene and Malhotra 2003; Ensminger and Knight 1997). Moreover, poverty not only contributes to increasing risk of early marriage, but also increases the likelihood that a girl will give birth at a young age, as child brides tend to have children early (Save the Children 2004).

Income generation, on the other hand, tends to protect girls from early marriage because families may be more willing to delay marriage when a girl is earning income (Jejeebhoy 1995; United Nations 1987). For example, only 31 percent of girls who left rural communities to work in the garment industry in Bangladesh married by 18, compared to 71 percent of girls who stayed home in these same communities (Amin, Diamond, Naved and Newby 1998; United Nations 1987).

Education

Similar to economic status, no or low educational status is a risk factor for child marriage, and higher educational status is protective. The focus here is on education as a protective factor. Studies strongly show that higher levels of schooling for girls decrease their risk of child marriage (NRC/IOM 2005; UNICEF 2005).

Girls with eight or more years of education are less likely to marry young than girls with zero to three years of school (NRC/IOM 2005). But even low levels of education can protect against early marriage. In a study of 42 countries, women between the ages of 20 and 24 who attended primary school were less likely to marry by 18 than women without a primary education. In Senegal, for instance, 20 percent of women with a primary school education married before 18, compared to 36 percent without a primary school education. The study found similar results for secondary education. For example, in Tanzania, women who attended secondary school were 92 percent less likely to be married before age 18 than women who attended only primary school (UNICEF 2005).

Education is widely credited as the most significant factor for delaying girls' age at marriage (Mathur, Greene and Malhotra 2003; United Nations Commission on Population and Development 2002). Over the last several decades, parents have come to value education for their children, and to be willing to postpone the marriages of their daughters so they can attain a higher education level (Schuler et al. 2006). It is thought that education enhances girls' autonomy, giving them negotiation skills in choosing a partner and influencing the timing of marriage (Lloyd and Mensch 1999; NRC/IOM 2005). Education also is believed to increase girls' aspirations and extend the process of finding a suitable marriage partner (Lloyd and Mensch 1999).

Other Potential Risk and Protective Factors

Though poverty and education have been well-investigated, evidence is scarce for other possible risk or protective factors that might help policy-makers and program practitioners target new efforts to prevent child marriage. Research on current programs addressing child marriage—where they are and whether they are effective— is also limited.

Age Gap

Research shows that girls who marry before 18 are more likely to be married to much older men (Mensch 1986; Mensch, Bruce and Greene 1998; NRC/IOM 2005). Significant spousal age gaps initially may appear inherent to the practice of child marriage because girls are younger when they marry as children than as women. But the age gap between partners in fact occurs not only because girls are younger, but also because men who marry child brides are more likely to be older than men who marry adult women (NRC/IOM 2005).

Though age gap and early marriage are strongly associated, the nature of this association is not understood. Age gap is regarded as a measure of equity between a woman and her partner. A smaller age gap indicates a higher status level for women (Amin and Cain 1997). Girls with much older husbands are less able to negotiate or make household decisions due to their lower status, which is a result of their younger age (NRC/IOM 2005).

This lower status, in turn, increases the likelihood that they will experience domestic violence and abuse (Kishor and Johnson 2004). Literature on the age gap between unmarried girls and older partners explains similar power dynamics that limit girls' ability to negotiate (Luke and Kurz 2002).

The largest age gaps between spouses in the world are found in sub-Saharan Africa and the Middle East. In central and western Africa, one-third of young women in first marriages report that their partner is 11 or more years older than themselves (NRC/IOM 2005).

Further research on age gap is needed. Whether early marriage is a consequence or predictor of early marriage is not understood. It also is unclear how decisions about spouse selection are made, particularly how a woman's higher level of bargaining power with a man closer to her own age is weighed with the financial security of an older man.

Polygyny

Polygyny, a union in which a husband has multiple wives, is strongly associated with age gap (NRC/IOM 2005; UNICEF 2005) because a husband's age is higher with each additional marriage. Countries with high rates of polygyny, such as those in West Africa, also have the highest age gaps in the world.

This relationship may exist because men who marry multiple women must acquire bride wealth before each marriage (NRC/IOM 2005). For the girl's family, the related financial benefits and social prestige of polygyny are often deemed more important than the disadvantages of marrying the girl at a young age to a much older man (Blanc and Gage 2000). The combined association of age gap and polygyny with early marriage requires further study.

Regional Factors within Countries

Though data is available on the variation of child marriage prevalence within countries, the literature appears to provide no evidence on whether or how regional differences within countries are associated with child marriage. This area of study is new and requires investigation. More is known about the association between an urban or rural residence and age at marriage. The literature indicates that living in rural areas increases the likelihood of marrying early. Girls in rural residences are more likely to marry 1.5 years younger than girls in urban areas (Westoff 2003).

Natal Family Characteristics

Evidence is inadequate on the effect of a girl's natal family circumstances and a community's marriage customs and practices on age at marriage. The literature recognizes that a range of factors affect natal home decision making on when and whom a girl marries. What remains unclear is what these factors are and how they are associated with age at marriage (NRC/IOM 2005).

Researchers speculate that these decisions are based on economic gains from marriage, including bride wealth, dowry and removal of a family's financial responsibility toward a girl; cultural norms related to marriage and gender roles; social status gained from marriage; perceived protection of girls from rape and disease via marriage; available education and income-generating opportunities for girls; age gap; polygyny; and wife ranking in a polygynous household (NRC/IOM 2005; Mathur, Greene and Malhotra 2003).

Some of these indicators are difficult to measure quantitatively. Qualitative research could deepen our understanding, but is currently limited. Literature is also scarce on the relationship between age at marriage and other natal home characteristics, including childhood place of residence, number of siblings, religion, ethnicity, socioeconomic status of the natal family and education of parents.

A better understanding of these factors could explain which parents make decisions to marry their daughters early, and provide a basis for further research on how and why these decisions are reached.

Existing Programs

Because the causes of child marriage are complex, varied and often interlinked, another way to understand and address the issue is by examining existing efforts that address child marriage both at the policy and program level. Though individual program examples often are cited, the literature lacks evidence of current practices working to increase the age at marriage, including where programs are and what approaches are being used, particularly in high prevalence countries. Recent literature calls for filling this gap so best practices can be created, scaled up and replicated (NRC/IOM 2005).

CONCLUSION

Most research on child marriage has focused on the prevalence and consequences of marrying young. Much less is understood about risk and protective factors for child marriage, which would provide important, evidence-based points for policy and program intervention. Also scarce is documentation on the current range and type of programmatic efforts by which best practices can be created, scaled up and replicated. This report aims to contribute actionable information on risk and protective factors for child marriage and on existing programs to combat it.

ANALYSIS OF DEMOGRAPHIC AND HEALTH SURVEYS (DHS) DATA

Methodology

This analysis investigates possible risk and protective factors for early age at marriage. Understanding these factors may provide intervention points for policymakers and development practitioners to change the course of a girl's future by delaying age at marriage and thus the negative consequences of marrying early. The analysis used datasets available from Demographic and Health Surveys (DHS), which carries out nationally representative household surveys that help governments and other interested parties monitor the population and health situation within countries. Standardized questionnaires allow for a fairly straightforward comparison of a range of indicators across countries.

The analysis reported here examines data from a women's questionnaire, which includes interviews with all women ages 15 to 49 who either resided in the household or visited the household the night before the survey was conducted in each country. However, DHS does not provide data on all countries in which child marriage is highly prevalent, such as some countries in the Middle East and Latin America, nor does it have data on all factors that may be associated with child marriage. Thus this analysis is limited to countries, survey years and indicators available from DHS.

The analysis considered factors associated with child marriage in 19 of the top 20 countries with the highest prevalence that were identified through 145 DHS surveys representing 68 countries. These 20 "hotspot" countries (Table 3.1) were determined by examining data on women ages 20 to 24 who married before 18. This ranking of hotspot countries is based on the most current year that survey information was available for each country.

Table : Top 20 "Hotspot" Countries for Child Marriage

Rank	Country	% Women Married < 18
1	Niger (1998)	76.6
2	Chad (2004)	71.5
3	Bangladesh (2004)	68.7
4	Mali (2001)	65.4
5	Guinea (1999)	64.5

Contd...

Rank	Country	% Women Married < 18
6	CAR (1994/95)	57.0
7	Nepal (2001)	56.1
8	Mozambique (2003)	55.9
9	Uganda (2000/01)	54.1
10	Burkina Faso (2003)	51.9
11	India (1998/99)	50.0
12	Ethiopia (2000)	49.1
13	Liberia (1986)	48.4
13	Yemen (1997)	48.4
15	Cameroon (2004)	47.2
16	Eritrea (2002)	47.0
17	Malawi (2000)	46.9
18	Nicaragua (2001)	43.3
18	Nigeria (2003)	43.3
20	Zambia (2001/02)	42.1

Source: ICRW analysis using MEASURE DHS STATcompiler.

Fifteen of the hotspot countries were in sub-Saharan Africa, three in South Asia, one in Central America and one in the Middle East. In sub-Saharan Africa, eight countries have more than 50 percent of women experiencing child marriage; five of these countries are in West Africa.

Empirical Strategy

The analysis sought to determine what factors might increase the risk of or serve as protection against child marriage in hotspot countries. That is, what household, individual and community characteristics are associated with increased or decreased age at marriage in these countries?

The outcome variable of interest was age at first marriage. The study only obtained data for women who had completed the survey and who were currently or had ever been in a union (i.e., married, living with someone, widowed, divorced or separated) at the time of the interview. While DHS data generally are available for women ages 15 to 49, the sample was restricted to women between 20 and 24 to capture a more recent account of child marriage. Age at marriage was measured both as a continuous variable and a bivariate variable, comparing women who married before 18 to women who married at 18 or older.

Primary Analysis

Binomial logistic regression was selected as the primary way to test the effect of the independent variables on age at marriage (younger than 18 versus age 18 and older) for a number of reasons. The study used cross-sectional data, did not look at any observations over time, and used explanatory variables that are not normally distributed. Additionally, logistic regression does not assume linearity between dependent and independent variables nor does it assume homoscedas-ticity. Generally, logistic regression has more flexible requirements suited to the variables of interest. Logistic regression also offers prevalence results with a cut-off age, which is a simple and convenient way to make comparisons both within and across countries, albeit with less statistical power than ordinary least squares (OLS). Results are reported as a ranking of the relative importance of independent variables in explaining the dependent variable.

Secondary Analysis

The study also used stepwise OLS regression for a multivariate model with age at marriage as a continuous variable. The forward stepwise option, which adds one variable at a time to the model, is useful because it estimates the strength of association with the dependent variable that an independent variable brings to the analysis when added to the regression model. This allowed comparison of results in broad terms to the logistic regression because both methods provide a ranking of the relative importance of the independent variables.

Tipping Point Analysis

A third analysis used logistic regression with a cut-off age called the "tipping point." This is the age at which the frequency of child marriage first increases significantly in a given country. The regression compared girls who married below the tipping point age with girls who married at or after the tipping point. The stark contrast between the number of girls who marry at the median age at marriage (age 15) and the tipping point age (age 13), or the age at which the frequency of child marriage first starts increasing significantly in Bangladesh. While 14.4 percent of girls married at 15, significantly more— 22.1 percent—married at 13.

An analysis of the tipping point reveals risk and protective factors of child marriage for younger girls who marry well before the median age at marriage, and how these factors differ from those of older girls. This analysis could be useful for programs seeking to prevent child marriage before it first begins to be a significant problem in a country.

In the tipping point regression analyses, as well as the primary and secondary analyses, variables were examined for problems with multicollinearity, sample size, ratio of cases to variables, missing cases and outliers. The linear regressions were further inspected for problems with linearity, heteroscedasticity and normality.

Table : Tipping Point Age Versus Median Age at Marriage

Country	Median age at marriage	Tipping point age at marriage
Mozambique	17	13
India	17	13
Cameroon	17	13
Zambia	17	14
Uganda	17	14
Malawi	17	14
Burkina Faso	17	15
Ethiopia	16	12
Nigeria	16	13
Nicaragua	16	13
Mali	16	13
Liberia	16	13
Yemen	16	14
Nepal	16	14
CAR	16	14
Niger	15	13
Guinea	15	13
Chad	15	13
Bangladesh	15	13

Variables and Model

The study sought to determine what factors were associated with age at marriage across hotspot countries. It also examined how these associations ranked in strength, or whether they were strongly, moderately or not at all correlated with a girl's age at marriage. Table 3.3 defines and describes dependent and independent variables in the model.

Economic status was calculated using a wealth index, an indicator created by DHS that is a composite measure of a household's living standard. This cumulative living standard is based on select assets owned by the household. It uses principal components analysis to generate quintiles—poorest, poorer, middle, richer and richest—that place households on a continuous scale of relative wealth. A wealth index was available in six of the 20 countries. In the remaining 13 countries, whether or not the marital home had electricity was used as a proxy for the wealth index.

The education variables for the respondent and her partner measured the highest education level attended in four categories: no education, primary, secondary and higher. These were constructed into six dummy variables—primary, secondary and higher education, using 'no education' as a reference—for both the respondent and her partner. This allowed the analysis to specify exactly what level of education might be associated with age at marriage.

The age gap variable was constructed as the age difference between a respondent and her partner. The analysis tests whether the younger age of a girl is associated with a greater difference in age between her and her partner.

The remaining variables—polygyny, region, type of place of residence, work prior to marriage, childhood place of residence, number of other siblings, religion and ethnicity—were constructed.

Some variables that may be associated with age at marriage, such as having a say in spouse selection or the education of girls' parents, were not available for the hotspot countries. Because of the unavailability of data or reasonable proxies, these factors that may affect age at marriage were not controlled for in the model. Additionally, because wife ranking, or the position of a wife among other wives in a polygynous household, was highly correlated with polygyny and had a high number of missing values in every dataset, it was dropped from the analysis. In sum, the model in this analysis looks at the effect of 12 different factors associated with age at marriage. The model varies slightly by country, depending on the availability and significance of explanatory variables. See Appendix 3 for a list of variables analyzed by country.

Subnational Analysis

In hotspot countries where the region variable was significant, further analysis was conducted to determine what factors were associated with child marriage in the region(s) with the highest prevalence.

Findings

For each hotspot country, the study conducted regression analysis of factors associated with child marriage. This section presents findings. First, it offers detailed logistical analysis results15 from Bangladesh and Mozambique to show how the analyses were conducted by country. These two countries were chosen because they are fairly typical of all hotspot countries. It then provides an overview of all results by factor, describing which factors were associated with child marriage across all hotspot countries. Finally, it discusses each individual factor in more detail. Though the effect of variables on child marriage is described individually, all results are from multivariate models.

Factors Associated with Child Marriage by Country: Bangladesh and Mozambique

At 68.7 percent, Bangladesh has the third highest prevalence of child marriage in the world, the highest rate outside of Africa. In Bangladesh, the post-primary education of a respondent is the most significant factor associated with whether a girl will marry before 18, which corresponds with findings across the hotspot countries. Age gap, wealth, post-primary education of the partner and religion were also significantly associated-with age at marriage, similar to other hotspot countries.

Mozambique, which is ranked eighth on the hotspot list, has a child marriage prevalence of 55.9 percent.

Region was the most important factor associated with child marriage in Mozambique, which indicates that knowing where child marriage occurs within the country is crucial to addressing the problem. Other significant factors were age gap and the secondary education of both the respondent and her partner. These results are typical of the other hotspot countries.

Major Associated Factors Across Countries

Analysis results showed a set of factors explaining child marriage across hotspot countries. These results were categorized based on the number of countries in which they were significant and their relative level of significance. The factors, in order of significance, were: (1) education of girls, (2) age gap, (3) region, (4) wealth, (5) religion, (6) education of the partner (secondary and higher) and (7) polygyny. Figure 3.3 shows the number of countries in which each of these variables is statistically significant. For example, secondary education of the respondent is significant in 17 of the hotspot countries, age gap in 12, and higher education of the respondent in 10. The remaining independent variables in the model—type of place of residence, childhood place of residence, ethnicity and number of siblings—were either not found to be significant or significant only in a few countries.

Education of Girls

Using logistic regression (age 18), girls' education was the most important factor associated with girls marrying before 18. Across the hotspot countries, secondary education was a significant factor in 17 countries, higher education in 10 countries and primary education in-nine countries. Comparing results on education across the three analyses shows that the logistic and the linear regression results for marriage before 18 were similar to each other. However, the tipping point logistic regression results are different, which would be expected for factors associated with marriage occurring at a much earlier age. For example, secondary education is significant in 17 countries with the former two regressions, but only in seven with the tipping point regression.

Higher education showed a similar difference between the logistic and linear regressions on the one hand and the tipping point regression on the other. However, the difference between results was more subtle with primary education: Logistic, linear and tipping point regression results showed significance in nine, 11 and eight countries respectively. Comparing the top three most significant factors for each country tells a similar story for these three levels of education.

These differences indicate that higher levels of education are more important for older rather than younger girls in delaying age at marriage.17 That is, post-primary rather than primary education can help older girls marry at 18 or later. But for girls who are around the tipping point age, primary education is a stronger influence on whether she will marry at this younger age.

Age Gap

Age gap between girls and their spouses was the second most important factor found to be associated with whether a girl would marry at a young age. That is, a large age difference between a girl and her partner was strongly associated with child marriage, whereas girls marrying at

18 or older had smaller differences in age with their husbands. In countries where age gap is prevalent, younger brides tend to have much older husbands.

Table : Median Age Gap and Age Gap Ranges by Country

Country	Median Age Gap	Highest Age Gap
Guinea	12	78
Niger	10	78
Mali	10	77
Nigeria	10	57
Chad	9	75
Burkina Faso	9	72
Bangladesh	9	50
Cameroon	7	59
Ethiopia	7	45
CAR	6	78
Uganda	5	78
India	5	78
Malawi	5	78
Yemen	5	73
Mozambique	5	52
Zambia	5	42
Nicaragua	4	51
Nepal	4	23
Liberia*	–	–

* Data on age gap not available for Liberia.

Age gap was a significant factor for child marriage in 12 countries, both with logistic and linear regression. Importantly, it was also significant in eight countries using the tipping point logistic regression. This indicates that age gap is an important factor for both younger and older girls.

Some hotspot countries, particularly in West Africa and Bangladesh, were also found to have large median age gaps. Dramatic age gap ranges appeared in nearly all of the countries. Women from 10 countries reported that their partners were as much as 70 years older than themselves.

Region

Regional differences were, for the most part, either the most important factor associated with child marriage in a country, or not important at all. Region was significant in nine of the hotspot countries using logistic regression and the most significant factor in seven of these countries.

Similarly, it was the most important factor in four of the five countries in which it was significant with the tipping point logistic regression. This all-or-nothing feature of regional differences indicates that, when significant, understanding where high levels of child marriage occur within a country and targeting these areas is crucial. Further analysis on high prevalence regions is presented in section 3.2.4, "Results at the Subnational Level."

Economic Status

Economic status is an important influence on age at marriage for both younger and older girls. The wealth variable, and the variable electricity where wealth was unavailable, was significant in eight, 11 and five of the hotspot countries using the logistic, linear and tipping point logistic regressions, respectively.

Similar to the region variable, its significance tended to be all or nothing. That is, in logistic regressions, it was either one of the two most important factors associated with child marriage in a country, or it was much less significant. Surprisingly, the analysis for some countries indicated that wealth was not a significant factor.

This may be because poverty is not as strong a variable as other indicators for some countries. Also, this model may have underestimated the strength of wealth's association with child marriage in several ways. First, wealth and electricity are only proxies for, but not perfect measurements of, poverty and economic status. A different measurement may have produced a stronger relationship with age at marriage. Also, in countries where it was the second most important factor, it was preceded only by the region variable, pointing to the fact that, though not highly multicollinear, wealth and region co-vary. Thus, the effect of wealth on age at marriage may have been captured by region as well as education and place of residence.

Religion

Table: Significance of Religion on Child Marriage by Country and Religious Affiliation

Country	Rank of significance	Religious affiliations
Chad	1	Muslim/Non-Muslim
Malawi	1	Catholic/Church of Central Africa, Presbyterian/Anglican/Seventh Day Advent-Baptist/Other Christian/Muslim/No religion/ Other
Cameroon	2	Catholic/Protestant/Muslim/Animist/Other/ No Religion/New Religions
Nigeria	2	Catholic/Protestant/Other Christian/Islam/ Traditionalist/Other
Burkina Faso	3	Muslim/Non-Muslim
Ethiopia	3	Orthodox/Muslim/Protestant/Other
India	5	Hindu/Non-Hindu
Bangladesh	6	Muslim/Non-Muslim

Religion was significant in eight countries both with logistic and linear regression, and it was significant in five countries using the tipping point regression. However, the analysis found that no one religious affiliation was associated with child marriage across countries. That is, a variety of religions were associated with high prevalence of child marriage, depending on the country.

These results indicate that targeting a particular religion across countries is not an effective way to address early marriage. In countries where religion was significant, further analyses are needed to better understand the relationship between religion and age at marriage.

Post-primary Education of the Partner

Though the post-primary education of partners influences age at marriage, it is less significant than other factors, such as the education of a girl. The secondary education of a partner is significant in nine and seven countries using logistic and linear regressions, respectively, and in six and eight countries for higher education of a partner.

These variables are not highly ranked and not among the most important factors in any country. Also, secondary and higher education of the partner are significant in only a few countries with the tipping point regression, indicating that addressing the post-primary education of partners is unlikely to have a major effect on younger girls' likelihood of marrying early.

Polygyny

Analysis results vary greatly by regression type for polygyny. Though results for linear regression are usually similar to those for logistic regression, polygyny is an exception. It is significant in seven countries in linear regression, but only once in logistic regression with age 18, and in three countries with the tipping point regression.

This difference between the two logistic regressions may indicate that polygyny is a more important factor for girls who marry at a much younger age.-That is, the younger a girl is married, the more likely she is to have a husband with multiple wives.

Interestingly, wherever polygyny is significant, age gap is not, signifying that polygyny may be capturing the variance of age gap in these countries. In other words, age gap and polygyny are so closely associated that the significance of either in a country may actually represent a combination of both.

Minor Variables

Primary school education of a partner, the respondent's childhood and current place of residence (urban versus rural), ethnicity, and number of siblings were significant in only a few countries and then only at low levels. The effects of these variables may have been captured by other variables or may not be strongly associated with age at marriage. Working prior to marriage was not found to be a significant factor for age at marriage, though data for this indicator was only available in Yemen.

Results at the Subnational Level

Understanding child marriage at the country level is not enough. Prevention efforts must recognize regional differences because prevalence and factors associated with child marriage may vary within a country.

The analysis looked within each hotspot country to determine where the highest levels occur and whether these regional differences are statistically significant. Where the national-level analyses found region to be significant, further analyses examined the factors associated with early age at marriage at the subnational level.

Table : Are Regional Differences within Countries Significant?

Yes, Regional Differences	No, Prevalence Consistent Across Regions
Country	Country
Burkina Faso	Bangladesh
Ethiopia	Cameroon
India	Central African Republic
Mali	Chad
Mozambique	Guinea
Nepal	Liberia
Nicaragua	Malawi
Uganda	Niger
Zambia	Nigeria
	Yemen

For countries with regional differences, lists the subnational regions that have the highest prevalence of child marriage for each country, as well as associated factors for age at marriage in these regions. Comparing factors associated with early marriage across countries versus within a country provides some insight into how high prevalence regions match up against the country as a whole. For example, subnational results for countries where region is significant tend to mirror the most important factors at the national level, such as post-primary education for older girls and primary education for younger girls.

But the subnational analysis tends to lose other factors, such as age gap, which was significant at the national level in four of the countries but at the sub-national level in only one of the countries. Similarly, all three of the countries in which wealth was significant at the national level did not find it significant at the subnational level. Finally, higher education, both of the respondent and her partner, was significant at the national level in four and two countries, respectively. Nicaragua was the only country where higher education, for respondents only, was significant at the subnational level. To explore these findings further, regional differences are examined in detail for two countries: Ethiopia and India. Both countries had large differences in child marriage prevalence within the country, and analysis results showed region as an important factor associated with age at marriage. Both also illustrate that there can be important differences between associated factors at the country level and those at the subnational level.

Ethiopia

In Ethiopia, 48 percent of child marriage occurs in the northern regions of the country, with prevalence in Amhara at 90 percent, Tigray at 82 percent, Afar at 77 percent and Benishangul (Ben-Gumuz) at 75 percent. Analysis results revealed that regional differences were highly associated with the age at which a girl married. Further analysis of the northern regions indicates that secondary education, religion, age gap and ethnicity are important factors for when a girl will marry. This holds true across the three types of regressions, with the exception of age gap, which is not significant for the tipping point logistic regression. These results point to ethnicity as an additional significant factor in the northern regions, an important distinction in understanding child marriage within the northern regions versus the country as a whole.

India

Five states in India have the highest prevalence of child marriage: Madhya Pradesh at 73 percent, Andhra Pradesh at 71 percent, Rajasthan at 68 percent, Bihar at 67 percent and Uttar Pradesh at 64 percent. Logistic regression using a cut-off age of 18 showed that region is a significant factor associated with age at marriage.

Table : Logistic (< 18 vs. > 18) Regression Results for Effect of Associated Factors on Child Marriage in India[a]

Variable[b,c]	Parameter Estimate	Odds Ratio	CI (95 %) Lower	Upper	P (ChiSq)
Higher education of the respondent	777.434	16.182	13.306	19.680	.006
Secondary education of the respondent	733.550	3.679	3.348	4.042	.000
Age gap	125.514	.949	.941	.958	.000
Primary education of the respondent	97.551	1.662	1.503	1.839	.000
Religion	55.921	1.391	1.276	1.517	.000
Wealth/electricity	51.432	1.350	1.243	1.465	.000
Secondary education of the partner	43.538	1.414	1.276	1.567	.000
Higher education of the partner	28.258	1.433	1.255	1.636	.000
Type of place of residence	18.831	.825	.756	.900	.000
Region	7.701	1.006	1.002	1.011	.000
Primary education of partner	5.810	1.158	1.028	1.306	.016
Constant	55.572	.442	–.	–	.000

[a] Sample size = 15,387; only includes women who are currently or were ever married or living with someone, and who are between the ages of 20 and 24.

[b] –2 Log Likelihood: 17,854.897, $p<.0001$; Nagelkerke R-Squared:.264; Chi-Square statistic (11 DF): 3393.981, $p<.0001$

[c] The ethnicity variable was not significant in the model.

Andhra Pradesh was dropped from the subnational analysis to examine an area known as the BIMARU region, which includes Bihar, Madhya Pradesh, Rajasthan and Uttar Pradesh. This region has many similar development characteristics across states and is considered the least developed in the country on many criteria.

An analysis of the BIMARU region showed that, across all three regression types, the post-primary education of the respondent, type of place of residence, age gap, religion, post-primary education of the partner and primary education of the respondent were all significant factors associated with child marriage. The primary education of the partner was significant only in the tipping point logistic regression.

These results are very similar to the national analysis, with one exception: While electricity, as a proxy for wealth or socioeconomic status, was a factor of age at marriage at the national level, it is not significant in the BIMARU region. There may be several explanations for this difference. Electricity may not serve as a good proxy for wealth, or the effect of wealth may have been captured by other variables. It is also possible that there may be lower variation in socioeconomic status in this region, or perhaps wealth may not be a factor for when a girl will marry in the BIMARU states.

CONCLUSION

An analysis of hotspot countries indicates that certain factors—secondary and primary education, age gap, economic status, and region—are strongly associated with child marriage, and may be key areas to target prevention efforts. Secondary and primary education were found to have the strongest association with age at marriage, indicating that education at all levels could help both older and younger girls reach 18 before marrying. Age gap had the second strongest association, suggesting the need to help discourage the practice of marrying young girls to much older men.

Similarly, the strong association between child marriage and economic status indicates that increasing wealth and addressing poverty may change norms and decision making about a girl's age at marriage. Finally, the strong association between region and child marriage may indicate that high prevalence regions are where social norms perpetuating child marriage are the most entrenched.

Though religion as a whole was found to be associated with age at marriage in several countries, further analysis showed that no one religion had this association across all countries. Also, while polygyny was associated with child marriage, a better understanding of this relationship, and the combined effect of age gap and polygyny on age at marriage, is needed. Other variables examined—education of partner, the respondent's childhood and current place of residence, ethnicity and number of siblings—were significant in only a few countries.

SCAN OF PROGRAMS

A number of nongovernmental and community organizations are working to decrease child marriage prevalence in their communities, but little is known about what type of work that is taking place and where; what gaps are and are not being filled by this work; and which approaches are feasible, effective and efficient. This information is necessary to best determine how to focus new efforts, which best practices can be scaled up or replicated, and which groups and regions to target.

Methodology

ICRW conducted a global program scan including programs that directly or indirectly address child marriage.

Direct refers to programs that measure child marriage prevalence or median age at marriage as an outcome, while indirect refers to programs that found evidence of a decline in child marriage as a result of work on other issues. The program scan was conducted only on the Internet. The scan used more than 35 keywords and combinations of keywords in search engines, including but not limited to reproductive health; circumcision (FGM/FGC); fistula; HIV/AIDS; early childbearing; maternal mortality; adolescents; education; policy; law; poverty; rural-urban; rights; women's status; domestic violence; intimate partner violence; age gap; polygyny; and wife ranking.

Searches also targeted regions, with keywords including Afghanistan, Africa, Asia, Bangladesh, Egypt, Ethiopia, India, Latin America and Middle East. The scan also includes programs listed on the Web sites of organizations known to work on child marriage. Finally, the scan includes searches of online journals, publications and books for further references to child marriage-related programs.

Because the program scan is Internet-based and searched only for programs written in English, it excludes programs without a Web presence or those that did not turn up in keyword searches. That is, the scan likely missed programs that are small and have limited resources. The scan also is limited to groups that relate their efforts to child marriage outcomes, missing those that may be influencing rates of child marriage but not describing it as an outcome. For example, maternal health programs may provide services to married adolescents but often do not measure or report this as work with child brides.

Despite these limitations, the search provides important information on areas where child marriage is being addressed, the range of sectors addressing it and the programmatic approaches being used. The scan also offers some insight on gaps not being met by these programs and approaches. In particular, analysis of the program scan sought answers to the following questions:

- Where are child marriage programs?
- How are programs categorized?
- Who are programs targeting?
- Are programs reducing child marriage?
- What lessons can be drawn from existing programs?

These questions were answered by categorizing programs in a given topic and looking for gaps within that topic. Finally, to corroborate these results, we consulted child marriage experts with extensive knowledge of existing programs to determine how accurately the scan captured the number and types of programs currently in operation. They also helped fill in gaps where the scan missed areas of work.

Findings

Where are Child Marriage Programs?

The program scan located a total of 66 programs,[18] some of which operate in multiple countries, either directly or indirectly addressing child marriage. The scan found 49 programs in Africa, 34 in South Asia and four in other areas of the world. In five of the 20 countries with the highest child marriage prevalence—Cameroon, Chad, Central African Republic, Nicaragua and Yemen—no programs were found. In six other hotspot countries—Guinea, Liberia, Mali, Mozambique, Niger, and Zambia—only one program in each country was identified. This finding was particularly striking in the case of Niger, which has the highest prevalence rate in the world at 76.6 percent. Of the 30 countries where programs were found, 16 countries had only one program, 10 countries had between two and five programs, and four countries had more than five programs. Although Nicaragua is the only hotspot country in Latin America, the two programs found in Latin America were in Guatemala. These findings clearly reveal the need to harmonize program work to reduce child marriage with the countries most in need.

How Are Programs Categorized?

Programs were organized into seven broad categories and 17 subcategories to determine types of child marriage programs and areas addressed. Because many programs are multifaceted, each could be counted in multiple categories or subcategories. This multiple counting explains why percents reported here are greater than 100.

The scan found that most programs are trying to change the underlying social norms that in various ways perpetuate child marriage. Fifty-eight percent of programs educate family and community members, and 42 percent educate girls. The scan found few programs which focus on research or the evaluation of child marriage programs (8 percent), and only one program reported providing services for married girls.

Many of the program scan subcategories also seek to change social norms on the practice of child marriage, particularly through behavior change communication (BCC) and community involvement. BCC, a multi-level approach that delivers tailored messages through a variety of communication channels to promote riskreducing behavior, includes the education of families, communities and girls, as well as law and policy efforts.

Overall, the most common types of child marriage programs are community sensitization and awareness-raising (48 percent of all programs in the scan), followed by life skills education programs19 (20 percent of all programs in the scan) and social marketing/edutainment (20 percent of all programs in the scan).

*Table : Program Scan Results by Subcategories (66 Total Programs)**

Category/Subcategory	No.	%
Education for family & community	38	58
Community sensitization/awareness raising	32	48
Social marketing/edutainment	13	20
Education for girls	28	42
Life skills	13	20
Nonformal education	12	18
Livelihood/vocational skills	7	11
Formal education	7	11
Law & Policy	21	32
Legal mechanisms	10	15
Advocacy	8	12
Community mobilization	6	9
Policy	2	3
Economic opportunities	9	14
Income generation for girls	5	8
Monetary incentives for families	4	6
Safeguarding rights	8	12
Shelter/creating safe spaces	4	6
Keeping birth or marriage records	3	5
Other rights (e.g., education)	1	2
Research	5	8
Services to married girls	1	2

* Totals exceed 66 programs/100 percent because multifaceted programs are counted in more than one category/sub-category.

Though the quantitative analysis in the previous section does not have results on nonformal education because DHS surveys do not collect these data, the program scan shows that 18 percent of programs are nonformal education efforts.

Only 5 percent of programs keep birth or marriage records, which are used to enforce child marriage laws and measure child marriage rates; 3 percent develop local policies and implement national policies on child marriage at the local level; 2 percent ensure that girls who are pregnant or give birth during their school years continue their education; and 2 percent provide reproductive health services to married girls.

Overall, the range of subcategories points to the various motivations, approaches, sectors and subsectors addressing social norms on child marriage. This finding indicates that child marriage is an important issue for many development areas and offers multiple entry points for building current efforts.

Who are Programs Targeting?

Child marriage programs found in the program scan most frequently target families and communities to change child marriage outcomes (73 percent of all programs), while girls are targeted in 55 percent and policy-makers in 21 percent. Only two programs in the scan targeted married girls, whereas 23 programs (64 percent of all programs that target girls) focused on unmarried girls.

Eleven (31 percent) of the programs that are focused on girls targeted both married and unmarried girls. This indicates that married girls are rarely the sole focus of child marriage programs, despite their very different needs and concerns.

This may be because most programs in the scan are interested in preventing child marriage, not assisting those who have already experienced it.

Table: Programs by Target Audience

Program Target Group	No.	%
Targeting family and community	48	73
Targeting girls	36	55
Only marrieds	2	6
Only unmarrieds	23	64
Both marrieds and unmarrieds	11	31
Targeting policy-makers	14	21

Are Programs Reducing Child Marriage?

The programs scan was unable to answer whether existing programs are in fact reducing the prevalence of child marriage because evaluation results were not available for most of them. Of the 66 programs captured in the scan, reports on results were found in only about 10 percent of programs. Even fewer programs provided information on an evaluation, or how results were determined.

Without evaluation, it is not known whether child marriage programs are effective or if funds are spent efficiently. Program implementers can also use evaluation results to share lessons and create best practices, which can help them reduce child marriage incidence more effectively and strategically.

What Lessons Can be Drawn from Existing Programs?

Six child marriage experts familiar with current programmatic responses were consulted to better understand how accurately the program scan was able to capture what is occurring in the field. These experts provided their impressions on whether the number and types of programs found in the program scan were accurate, as well as where the scan may have missed areas of work on child marriage.

On the types of programs, two experts agreed that not many programs are targeting married girls, and another confirmed that education programs are numerous. One also noted that more income generation programs may be operating in the field than are represented in the scan, suggesting that many microfinance and SME (small and medium scale enterprise) activities are working with women so they can generate income, which helps delay marriage. Finally, the experts felt more information was needed about the various programmatic efforts to reduce child marriage, and whether they are effective. They confirmed the need for an expanded program scan to provide a systematic review of child marriage programs, and its usefulness to researchers and program implementers.

Examples of Existing Programs

Tostan Taps Tradition to Prevent Child Marriage Tostan, an international nongovernmental organization based in Senegal, uses a combination of nonformal education and social mobilization to advance its goal of empowering communities and reducing the practices of child marriage and female genital cutting (FGC). Local facilitators teach education sessions which include child marriage-related issues such as sexually transmitted infections, AIDS, birth control and birth spacing. Those who take part in the education program pass on their new knowledge to the rest of the community as well as to other villages through inter-village meetings.

Public discussions are held with the community to seek its support in denouncing harmful practices, including early marriage. The program also taps into African tradition—dance, poetry, theater and song—to convey messages and gain the buy-in of stakeholders, including girls who may be targeted for early marriage and people who have influence over those decisions. Tostan's model for peaceful social change is based on the belief that communities themselves must consciously and actively pursue the process of change from within. The program was able to bring about change in knowledge, attitudes and behaviors in 90 intervention villages, and these were reinforced by a public declaration by approximately 300 villages against child marriage and FGC.

Community Mobilization Key to Preventing Child Marriage

In the Aurangabad area of Maharashtra, India, girls typically married early, usually around age 14, and early childbearing followed shortly afterward. The Institute for Health Management, Pachod (IHMP) was concerned with the ill effects this had on girls' empowerment, maternal health, and ultimately family health and well-being. In response, they started year-long life skills programs for unmarried 11–17-yearold girls. IHMP worked closely with parents and leaders, and involved the communities in all aspects of the program.

The life skills course included individual projects carried out in the communities, local recruitment of teachers, and regular and planned meetings with parents. In the planning phase, mothers reported that it would be easier for them to overcome the social pressure to get their daughters married early if their daughters were in school. However, formal education beyond the 4th standard was unavailable in the communities, and they welcomed the life skills program as an alternative. After only one year of the program, age at marriage in the area increased from 16 to 17 years (Pande et al. 2006). This increase was a community-level result, not just among girls participating in the life skills classes themselves, a tribute to how the communities as a whole were mobilized to change the social norm around the age at marriage. 'Booking' Practice Substitutes School for Prospective Grooms In 1999, Christian Children's Fund's (CCF) Margery Kabuya started a program to prevent child marriage among Kenya's Maasai tribe through an approach that taps into Maasai traditions and compensates for the economic incentive of marrying girls.

In the Maasai culture, baby girls are promised as wives to men before they are even born—a practice called "booking." The project, called the Naning'oi Girls Boarding School, substitutes the traditional practice of booking girls for marriage with booking them for school instead. Naning'oi works within the framework of the dowry system, where the school represents a man in search of a young bride. Wellrespected members of the Maasai community become "suitors" on the school's behalf, offering gifts to a girl's father in exchange for committing to his daughter's attendance at the boarding school. To date, 350 girls are enrolled and more than 500 additional infants and girls have been booked, waiting until they are old enough to attend school.

Local Governance Efforts Prevent Child Marriage

In the Amhara region of Ethiopia, Berhane Hewan, a Population Council project, helps girls avoid early marriage by promoting functional literacy, life skills, reproductive health education and opportunities for saving money. The local Ministry of Youth and Sports staff, which developed this program, felt that efforts to reduce child marriage needed to focus on the economic incentives of marrying girls early. Accordingly, families were assisted financially so they could allow their daughters to participate in girls' groups and remain in school. The project has been enthusiastically embraced by the community, with more than 750 girls currently participating.

The program scan found few programs overall and few or none in most countries with a high prevalence of child marriage, revealing the need for more programs that target child marriage and better geographic matching of interventions with high prevalence countries, where services are most needed.

The scan also suggested that child marriage is an important issue for many development sectors, which offers multiple entry points for building current efforts. However, it also found that programs often work in isolation, indicating a need for better communication to share lessons learned and improve the efficiency of interventions. Additionally, few programs are evaluating the impact of their interventions, suggesting a role for funding program evaluations. Finally, the program scan revealed a need for services for married girls. Programs are mostly focused on prevention and so married girls are largely overlooked, despite their pressing needs and concerns.

RECOMMENDATIONS AND DISCUSSION

Programs, Evaluation and Research

The following recommendations provide new or reinforce existing insights into the best ways to prevent child marriage globally. These recommendations are based on the findings from this analysis of the Demographic and Health Surveys (DHS) datasets and the scan of programs that directly or indirectly address child marriage.

Promote Education and Economic Opportunities for Girls

The DHS analysis shows that girls' education is the most important factor associated with age at marriage. Secondary education specifically emerges as the strongest factor associated with lower rates of child marriage. For preventing the marriage of young girls at the "tipping point" age—the age at which child marriage prevalence in a country starts to increase markedly (usually 13 or 14), the analysis shows that keeping girls in primary school is the most important factor. The best program approach would be to promote all levels of education to ensure both younger and older girls reach 18 before they marry. Improving a family's economic status may play a role in reducing child marriage.

This means reducing poverty in the long term and, more immediately, providing economic opportunities for unmarried girls after they finish school. A girl's ability to earn income can help alleviate family poverty and provide girls, as well as their families, with the option to delay marriage. Programs and policies also should offset financial incentives for parents to marry daughters at a young age, for example, by making it easier for parents to afford education and by addressing norms on bride price and dowry, which implicitly encourage parents to marry off their young daughters.

Employ Behavior Change Communication and Community Mobilization Techniques to Change Social Norms of Age at Marriage

Behavior change communication (BCC) and community mobilization are an effective set of techniques for promoting social change. The program scan shows that these techniques, which promote community discussion about marriage, are commonly used as a means to influence norms that encourage or condone child marriage. As several of the programs highlight, social norms of age at marriage need to change for the practice and, therefore, the prevalence of child marriage to decrease. As such, BCC and community mobilization should be promoted and employed to both understand and change the social norms that perpetuate child marriage, and to ultimately reduce its practice and prevalence.

Ensure Programs Are Where Child Marriage Is Most Prevalent: The program scan shows that existing programs were concentrated in a few countries, and that many high prevalence countries had no programs to reduce child marriage. For instance, Niger has the highest prevalence of child marriage in the world, with more than 76 percent of girls marrying before 18; yet the program scan found only one program in the country. Such findings indicate the need to systematically target programs to hotspot countries, particularly if program resources are limited. It also underscores the need for more collaboration among existing programs. Opportunities to share lessons and create best practices can lead to broader, more strategic efforts and help to improve child marriage interventions where the practice is most prevalent. The DHS analysis further reveals that some hotspot countries have clearly identified regions in which child marriage is significantly more prevalent. In these countries, such as Ethiopia and India, targeting approaches to the highest prevalence regions should help maximize the efficiency of child marriage prevention efforts. One caveat, however, is that key factors associated with child marriage at the country level are not necessarily identical to the key factors within a particular region.

This was the case in Ethiopia, for instance, where ethnicity was a key factor associated with child marriage in the north, but not in the country as a whole. This suggests that interventions appropriate for a country as a whole may differ from region-specific interventions. Thus, programs designed for a particular region should be tailored to the specific conditions and situation in that region.

Identify and Evaluate Existing Child Marriage Programs

The scan of programs that address child marriage yielded only 66 programs worldwide. The information gleaned from this scan is an important first step in gathering quality information on child marriage programs, but it likely underestimates the true number of efforts to reduce child marriage. An expanded program scan that includes a focus on select countries would provide a clearer picture of what is happening on the ground. For example, interviews with a full range of program practitioners, policy-makers and advocates in high prevalence countries could shed light on other successful programs. These also could generate more detailed information on program content and motivation.

The program scan also revealed the need to evaluate child marriage programming. Few programs contained evaluations, making it impossible to know whether specific interventions increased the age at marriage. Funds are well-spent if programs achieve their intended results, and this knowledge can be assessed through evaluations.

Ongoing monitoring and evaluation provides important information to help program implementers revise and improve interventions as needed. Furthermore, ICRW research shows that costs of monitoring and evaluation can be contained to 20 percent or less of total program costs.

Monitoring and evaluation skills are not widespread, however. The development of evaluation guidelines that can be applied to a variety of programs, laws and government policies working to reduce the prevalence of child marriage is recommended. Guidelines should be dynamic, flexible and updated with the latest lessons learned for program monitoring and evaluation.

Conduct Further Research on Age Gap

The research on child marriage is still relatively new, and several issues demand further study. One area in particular is how the age gap between husbands and wives relates to child marriage. The analysis suggests that spousal age gap is likely to be greater for child brides and is strongly associated with early marriage. Further investigation is needed to explain why families choose or consent to a much older husband for their daughter, and to understand their perceptions of the negative consequences this age gap has for young girls.

Although it is unclear how age gap is associated with age at marriage, or which influences the other, programs can still address age gap by educating families and communities of its likely adverse effects on girls' well-being such as complications related to early pregnancy and childbirth. Interventions also can support efforts that postpone marriage, such as education and employment; women are more likely to marry men closer to their own age when they postpone marriage.

Address the Needs of Married Girls

This report and its recommendations focus on ways to prevent child marriage and reduce its prevalence throughout the developing world. However, until efforts to prevent child marriage are more successful, many girls will continue to be married and bear children while still young, which puts them at greater health risk for complications related to pregnancy and childbirth. In addition to prevention, therefore, child marriage efforts should promote the following services: family planning services to postpone the first birth and to increase spacing between children, earlier and more frequent use of maternal health services for young brides and their families, and other reproductive health and HIV services for prevention or treatment. Because adolescent girls are less likely than adult women to seek out such services, they require greater encouragement and community support. Programs also need to help young married women take advantage of education and economic opportunities.

U.S. Government

The U.S. government, with its strong record in funding international development work and its capacity to influence international policy, has a unique role to play in combating child marriage worldwide. By coordinating efforts among government agencies, helping to build in-country capacity to address child marriage and taking the lead in ensuring that valuable lessons learned from child marriage prevention work are shared as widely as possible, the U.S. government has the potential to be a key player in helping end this practice.

Invest in an Integrated Set of Program and Policy Initiatives

The program scan indicated that efforts to reduce the prevalence of child marriage span a variety of sectors (education, legal, economic, health) and approaches (program, laws and policy; advocacy; and awareness-raising at local and international levels). An integrated effort to address child marriage will improve the efficiency of programs to increase the age at marriage among young and adolescent girls. Relevant U.S. government agencies, initiatives and offices, such as USAID and the State Department's Women's Legal Empowerment Initiative and the Office of International Women's Issues, for example, could invest in an integrated set of child marriage program and policy initiatives to ensure that a range of sectors and approaches are addressed.

Child marriage also could be woven into other sectors within the USAID framework. For example, in the "Foreign Assistance Standardized Program Structure and Definitions," child marriage could be integrated within the Governing Justly and Democratically pillar, in human rights (program element 1.4); within the Investing in People pillar, in maternal and child health (program element 1.6), family planning and reproductive health (element 1.7), basic education (element 2.1); and within the Economic Growth pillar, in microenterprise productivity (element 7.3).

Build In-country Capacity for Conducting Program Evaluations

In-country programs need to invest in their capacity to conduct program evaluations. The U.S. government can help by investing in training and technical assistance to increase the number of in-country professionals who can appropriately monitor and evaluate programs, laws and government policies aimed at reducing child marriage.

Facilitate Cross-communication and Learning

U.S. government agencies with a field presence, such as USAID and the State Department, could create forums and opportunities to share program and advocacy designs, experiences and lessons learned from existing efforts to address child marriage. One way is to feature several long-running programs and advocacy efforts known to have reduced child marriage, such as Tostan from Senegal and the Institute of Health Management, Pachod, from India. Because the scaling up of programs is a relatively high-efficiency, low-cost strategy in program work, discussions on steps for scaling up successful, well-documented child marriage programs should be included from the outset of meetings to share lessons learned and next steps.

In countries where there is interest in combating child marriage, USAID could organize consultations among stakeholders to guide their process of prioritizing child marriage prevention and integrating it into other existing initiatives. The consensus from such consultations should be reflected in annual country operating plans and through investments in program and policy efforts to reduce child marriage.

4

THE LIVES, RIGHTS, AND HEALTH OF YOUNG MARRIED GIRLS

Millions of young girls in the developing world are married when they are still children, and as a result are denied the ordinary experiences that young people elsewhere take for granted: schooling, good health, economic opportunities, and friendship with peers. Despite national laws and international agreements forbidding early marriage, gender roles and marriage systems in many countries dictate the practice, through which girls are deprived of basic rights and subjected to discrimination and health risks.

Instead of being viewed as children or teenagers with potential and opportunities in their lives, girls are often defined by social custom solely as wives and mothers. This limited view exposes girls to responsibilities and risks that they are often not physically or mentally prepared to undertake, while at the same time disrupting their prospects for education and employment.

In addition to having a negative impact on girls themselves, the practice of early marriage also has negative consequences for children, families, and society as a whole.

Nearly all of the world's nations have concurred repeatedly that childhood-with the ongoing investment in the young person that the notion implies-should last until age 18. Many governments and a number of international agreements have also settled upon age 18 as the minimum legal age at marriage. This consensus reflects both an understanding of the adverse effects of bearing children at a young age, and the increasing recognition that secondary education and economic options are essential for young people to succeed in life and contribute to society.

The number and scope of international and national statements on early marriage and the laws that regulate the practice in most countries are extensive, making the degree to which they are disregarded even more startling. Significant proportions of girls marry before age 18 in countries, such as Mali, Bangladesh, Uganda, and Nicaragua, that have established 18 as the legal minimum age at marriage. The case of Cameroon provides an even more staggering example: although the legal minimum age at marriage for women is 21, 62 percent of women in their early 20s are already married before age 18, according to Demographic and Health Survey (DHS) data. In a number of countries (including the United States), marriage of girls may take place as early as 14 or 15 with the consent of parents.

THE GLOBAL PREVALENCE OF EARLY MARRIAGE

Worldwide, there are more than 51 million adolescent girls aged 15-19 who are married and bearing the burden of domestic responsibility and the risks associated with early sexual activity, including pregnancy.3 As Figure 1 shows, rates of early marriage are highest in West Africa, South Asia, and East and Central Africa, where approximately 30 percent or more of girls aged 15-19 are already married.4 Rates are also relatively high, but more moderate, in Central America and the Caribbean, where 20 percent of girls aged 15-19 are married, compared to 2-4 percent in North America, East Asia, and Western Europe.

United Nations Agreements on the Minimum Age at Marriage and Protection of Children from Sexual Exploitation

1948

The Universal Declaration of Human Rights states that "men and women of full age, without any limitation due to race, nationality or religion, have the right to marry and to found a family. They are entitled to equal rights as to marriage, during marriage and at its dissolution. Marriage shall be entered into only with the free and full consent of the intending spouses."

1962

The Convention on Consent to Marriage, Minimum Age for Marriage, and Registration of Marriages calls not only for the establishment everywhere of minimum ages at marriage for both boys and girls, but also for the official registration of those marriages as a public statement of the union and as a source of legal recourse if problems in the marriage arise.

1979

Convention on the Elimination of All Forms of Discrimination against Women confirms that "States parties shall take all appropriate measures to eliminate discrimination against women in all matters relating to marriage and family relations and in particular shall ensure, on a basis of equality of men and women: the same right to enter into marriage; the same right freely to choose a spouse and to enter into marriage only with their free and full consent; the betrothal and the marriage of a child shall have no legal effect, and all necessary action, including legislation, shall be taken to specify a minimum age for marriage and to make the registration of marriages in an official registry compulsory."

1989

The Convention on the Rights of the Child (CRC) defines children as people under the age of 18.

1994

The International Conference on Population and Development Programme of Action (PoA) refers specifically and repeatedly to the need to increase age at marriage. It recommends efforts to eliminate coercion and discrimination related to child marriage, to enforce minimum age at marriage laws, and to generate social support for these laws by providing educational and employment opportunities to girls and young women.

Regional patterns of early marriage are welldefined, but they hide considerable intraregional variation among countries. In Africa, there are countries with very high rates of early marriage, such as Niger (77 percent), Chad (71 percent), and Mozambique (57 percent), but others such as Togo in West Africa have a more moderate rate of early marriage (31 percent), while South Africa has a fairly small percentage of young women who marry early (8 percent). Similarly, countries in Asia show wide variation in rates of early marriage among young women.

For example, in South Asia, the rate is very high in Bangladesh (65 percent), moderately high in India (48 percent), and very low in Sri Lanka (14 percent). Compared to other parts of Asia, rates of early marriage are generally lower in Southeast and East Asia. For example, among young women in their early 20s, only 15 percent in the Philippines and 12 percent in Vietnam were married by age 18.

In the Middle East, Central Asia, and Latin America, where overall rates of early marriage are moderate, there is -also variation across specific countries. Proportions of women aged 20-24 who were married before age 18 range from 14 percent in Jordan, to 21 percent in the Kyrgyz Republic, to 48 percent in Yemen. Marriage statistics in Latin America often do not fully capture the extent of marriage-like cohabitation and consensual unions that are so common in the region. However, official marriage rates vary across countries in that region as well, from 54 percent in Nicaragua to 21 percent in Bolivia.

CAUSES OF EARLY MARRIAGE

> *Nobody [protests against early marriage] because all take daughters as a burden. They fear that their daughters might get involved with other boys and that is why they want their daughters to get married at an early age.-Respondent in a focus group of rural unmarried girls, Nepal 2000*

Historically, there have been two major motivations for marrying girls at very young ages. Since high mortality rates have existed for much of human history-especially high maternal and infant mortality rates-the marriage of girls at or near puberty has been important for maximizing fertility in socially sanctioned unions. Moreover, rarely has marriage been an affair between two individuals; early marriage of children was an important means for securing critical social, economic, and political alliances for the family, clan, or lineage. The world has changed radically since many of these institutional mechanisms and norms were established and, for the most part, such motivations have become much less important, if not obsolete. Mortality rates have declined sharply in the last century through much of the developing world and, in the last several decades, fertility rates have also declined significantly.

In a globalizing world, numerous mechanisms have supplanted marriage for the purposes of social, economic, and political influence or alliance-building. However, established norms and social structures that encourage the marriage of young girls have been difficult to change in many societies and have been most tenacious where demographic and socioeconomic change have been slowest.

GENDER ROLES AND A LACK OF ALTERNATIVES

Adolescence-the juncture between childhood and adulthood-is a period when both boys and girls face a number of pressures to adjust to, explore, and experience life as their culture defines it. In many societies, boys face social and cultural pressures during adolescence to succeed in school, prove their sexuality, engage in sports and physical activity, develop a social group of peers, and demonstrate their ability to shoulder household economic and financial responsibilities. Rarely do these pressures translate into early marriage for boys.

In contrast, the adolescent experience of girls in many developing countries may be defined almost entirely in terms of entry into the marital state; emphasis is placed on domestic work and obedience, traits seen as essential to being good wives and mothers.

The wider range of developmental activities, including schooling, skill building, sports, and friendships, are often not part of the adolescent experience of girls because marriage is on their immediate horizon.

Research on age at marriage in different cultures and ethnic and religious groups suggests that getting married and bearing children are often the only means for young girls to secure identity and status in families and as adults in society. The more central the role of wife and mother is to women's identities-and the fewer alternative social and economic activities that are available-the earlier girls will tend to marry (Okonofua 1995 and Gage 1998).

In most countries, a significantly higher proportion of young women aged 15-19 is currently married when compared to young men of the same age group. This ratio is not only extremely skewed in countries where girls marry very early, such as Mali (72:1), but in other countries as well; for example, it is 8:1 in the United States and 6:1 in El Salvador (Alan Guttmacher Institute 1998). With a few exceptions, it is therefore mostly girls, not boys, who enter the marital state during, or even before, their teen years.

It is important to note that prevailing gender roles can limit the full impact of educational or employment opportunities for girls. For example, research in Bangladesh shows that parents pull daughters out of school because of expectations that husbands should be better educated than wives (Arends-Kuenning 2000).

Research in Nepal shows that although young people and their parents aspire to having daughters experience education, careers, and delayed marriage and childbearing, they find it difficult to go against social custom, which stigmatizes girls who break existing norms by engaging in activities that delay marriage and childbearing (Mathur, Malhotra, and Mehta 2001).

Value of Virginity and Fears about Premarital Sexual Activity

In many cultures around the world, a woman's sexuality is not her own to control, but the property of her father, husband, family, or ethnic group. Because of this, the decision to marry-and to initiate sexual activity-is often not a young woman's but that of family members, whose honor and shame are defined by whether or not she is a virgin before she marries. Once a girl has menstruated, fears of potential pre-marital sexual activity and pregnancy become the major concern among family members who are accountable for "protecting" her sexuality.6 Thus, the timing of a girl's first menstruation is associated with the first steps toward marriage in many settings.

Research shows that young married girls' understanding of their bodies and sexuality is often severely limited by the importance placed on virginity in their cultures (Dowsett et al. 1998). Adolescents in Brazil report that negative repercussions from losing one's virginity include hurtful gossip, pressure from boys to have sex, and being socially ostracized (Vasconcelos et al. 1995).

In Bangladesh, parents feel the pressure to marry their daughters early out of fear that a girl may make an unsuitable match of her own or that malicious gossip will circulate about her and spoil her chances for a good marriage (Huq and Amin 2001). In the event that premarital sexual activity does occur and results in pregnancy, many young people find themselves thrust into early marriages. Research from Indonesia and northeastern Brazil suggests that marriage sometimes provides the only acceptable solution to a pregnancy that occurs outside of marriage (Bennett 2001 and Gupta 2000).

Marriage Alliances and Transactions

Pressure to use marriage to reinforce family, caste, and tribal linkages-which in turn create political, economic, and social alliances-tends to lower the age at marriage in a variety of settings (Chandrasekhar 1996 and Hussain 2001). For example, in Yemen the growth in marriage among relatives has contributed to a lower age at marriage for women (Jurdi and Saxena 2003). Moreover, in most cultures around the world, economic transactions are integral to the marriage process, with an underlying assumption that these costs are lower when marriage occurs at an early age.

In Bangladesh, for example, dowry increases in tandem with age at marriage, placing pressure on parents to marry their daughters early.

This may be especially true if the family or the bride suffers from other disadvantages in the marriage market (such as the lower social status of her family or darker skin tone) (Huq and Amin 2001).

In fact, the relatively recent introduction of dowry in such places as southern India and Bangladesh may be a factor in keeping the marriage age lower than it would be otherwise, given the degree of other social and economic changes that have occurred. In many African cultures, bridewealth7 signifies wives' obligation to bear children and to fulfill other duties and can reinforce their subordinate position in relation to husbands (Bawah et al. 1999). Like dowry, bridewealth can foster early marriage because it is when a girl is young that her productive labor and reproductive capacities are seen as "best buys" in exchange for valued cattle or other goods (Nasimiyu 1997).

The Role of Poverty

Poverty and low levels of development are also important reasons for the early marriage of girls. In families that are very poor, a daughter may be seen as an economic burden that must be shed through marriage as early as possible. Similarly, the economic gains incurred through the marriage of a daughter may also be an important motivating factor for poor families.

In settings as diverse as Ethiopia, India, and Malaysia, families cite economic reasons for marrying girls early. In Ethiopia, parents explicitly state that they married their daughters when they did for the purposes of economic gain or to relieve economic burden (Berhane-Selaisse 1993). In both Malaysia and India, poverty in general, but especially among those in the agricultural sector, is an important determinant of early marriage (Pandey 1984 and Anderson, Hill, and Butler 1987).

At the societal level, countries, states, and regions that are less developed and poorer tend to have fewer resources and a lower level of motivation for investing in alternative options for young girls. Early marriage is therefore more common than it is in richer and more developed settings, where investments in the lives of girls are commonplace. Generally, countries with higher levels of economic or social development tend to have higher average ages at marriage for women than countries that are poorer or lacking in social progress. Many studies show that aggregate levels of education and literacy, as well as community development, are positively associated with age at marriage (Prakasam and Upadhyay 1985, Ganiger 1992, and Tripathy, Rao, and Pradhan 1992). Research suggests that this is because of greater social acceptability of unmarried girls and young women, as well as young girls' own aspirations for other experiences and ambitions in life before entering marriage.

CONSEQUENCES OF EARLY MARRIAGE

Early marriage contributes to a series of negative consequences both for young girls and the societies in which they live. Young married girls are at greater risk of reproductive morbidity and mortality. The timing of early marriage almost always disrupts girls' education, reducing their opportunities for future financial independence through work.

Young women are often married to men who are much older, and find themselves in new homes with greater responsibilities, without much autonomy or decision-making power, and unable to negotiate sexual experiences within marriage. This relative lack of power is associated with higher levels of violence in marriage and higher rates of unwanted pregnancy and sexually transmitted disease, including HIV/AIDS (Heise, Ellsberg, and Gottemoeller 2002). These impacts on young married girls subsequently contribute to negative consequences for their children, families, and societies.

Health and Related Outcomes

Early Childbearing, Unwanted Pregnancies, and Unsafe Abortions: Early marriage means early sexual activity, and therefore early childbearing. Despite the widespread recognition in societies and the medical community that childbearing during the adolescent years is harmful to both mother and child, it is a common phenomenon in large parts of the developing world. For example, in Uganda, 42 percent of women have given birth by age 18, whereas only 2 percent of women in France have done so. As Figure 3 shows, 24-45 percent of women in countries such as Guatemala, India, Mali, and Yemen have given birth by age 18, compared to only 1 percent in Germany and 2 percent in France. Recent research shows that most young married girls in developing countries do not want to bear children at such early ages.

Nor do they want to bear the burden of repeated pregnancies and large families while they are themselves still children. In many situations, young married girls are under pressure to demonstrate fertility soon after marriage and lack the personal autonomy to make decisions about their reproductive lives.8 Data from India shows that for these reasons, as well as the lack of options for effective temporary methods of contraception, significant proportions of young girls are either sterilized in their early 20s or resort to unsafe abortions (Malhotra et al. 2003).

Lack of Knowledge, Information, and Access to Services: Early marriage usually means that young girls enter marriage without adequate information about critical sexual and reproductive heath issues, such as sexual intercourse, contraception,- sexually transmitted diseases, pregnancy, and childbirth. For example, general awareness of HIV/AIDS and condoms is high in most countries, but among currently married 15-19-yearold girls, only 27 percent in Ethiopia, 40 percent in Malawi, and 40 percent in Haiti know that condoms can be used to prevent the disease. Even lower proportions of young married girls in these countries know that condoms can also be used to prevent pregnancy.

The negative consequences of a lack of information and knowledge are further compounded by a lack of access to services for pregnancy and disease prevention and proper antenatal and postnatal care. Social norms about what questions are acceptable for young girls to ask, restrictions on girls' mobility, and girls' lack of decision-making authority and resources in the marital home severely limit access to the services required to address reproductive health needs. Research in India, Nepal, and several African settings confirms the importance of the above factors in limiting access to services for young married girls. Research in India has also documented that decisions about whether young married girls seek health care when necessary are largely controlled by husbands and mothers-inlaw (Barua and Kurz 2001).

The provision of reproductive health services for young married couples is rarely a priority in most governmental or nongovernmental (NGO) programs. In fact, services are so explicitly tailored for older age groups that young married girls are among the most underserved clientele. Many service providers-including doctors, nurses, midwives, and traditional birth attendants-do not recognize this age group as one in need of advice, information, or services. To the contrary, data shows that many health providers have highly judgmental and nonsupportive attitudes toward young people regardless of their marital status (Mensch, Bruce, and Greene 1998 and Singh and Samara 1998).

High Maternal Mortality and Morbidity: Underdeveloped physiology, combined with a lack of power, information, and access to services, means that young married girls experience much higher levels of maternal mortality and morbidity than do women who bear children when they are older. As Figure 4 shows for countries where data according to age is available, maternal mortality rates are significantly higher among younger than older women. In Mali, for example, the maternal mortality ratio (MMR) for women aged 15-19 is 178 per 100,000 live births, compared to an MMR of only 32 for women aged 20-34. The contrast in Togo is even sharper, with MMRs for these age groups of 286 and 39, respectively. In Guatemala, 15-19-year-olds have an MMR of 35, in contrast to an MMR of 5 for women aged 20-24. These divergent experiences, determined by age of the mother, persist even where maternal mortality is very low overall, as it is in developed countries such as the United States.

At young ages, health problems associated with pregnancy and childbirth are also more common. Morbidity levels among young mothers are very high, especially for severe complications such as obstructed labor or obstetric fistula, which is often a result of obstructed labor and occurs most commonly among young women (UNFPA and EngenderHealth 2003 and Jarrett 1994).9 If the obstructed labor is not interrupted in a timely manner, a fetus' head may push against a young woman's pelvis for days, cutting off blood supply and killing surrounding tissue. Such conditions often lead to the death of the baby and permanent morbidity (sometimes mortality) for the mother. Studies in Ethiopia show that obstructed labor accounts for 46 percent of maternal deaths and that three in 1,000 pregnant women develop fistula (UNFPA and EngenderHealth 2003). This problem is especially common among women giving birth for the first time (Gaym 2000). Obstetric fistula is not limited to Africa, however, but is also common in many countries, such as Bangladesh (Akhter, Chowdhury, and Sen 1996).

Increased Risk of Contracting Sexually Transmitted Diseases and HIV/AIDS: Young women generally enter into marriage with partners who are much older and more sexually experienced. In these marriages, women have little negotiating power in sexual behavior and practices, putting them at greater risk of contracting reproductive and sexually transmitted infections. Research from 16 countries in sub-9 Fistula is an abnormal link between the urinary tract or rectum and vagina that results in continuous leaking of urine and feces. Saharan Africa indicates that the husbands of 15-19-year-old girls are on average at least 10 years older than their wives (UNICEF 2001). In Kenya and Zambia, data shows that young married girls are more likely to be HIV-positive than their unmarried peers because they have sex more often, use condoms less often, are unable to refuse sex, and have partners who are more likely to be HIV-positive (Clark 2003 and Luke and Kurz 2002).

Thus, evidence gained from research disproves the belief that early marriage may protect young women from HIV/AIDS. Moreover, comparative research on cross-generational sex corroborates that in partnerships with older men, adolescent women have very little control over sexual relations because of the risk of violence and the sense of obligation incurred by dependency on gifts or other forms of economic exchange (Luke and Kurz 2002).

Life Outcomes

Lack of Opportunity, Skills, and Social Support: With regard to access to educational and economic opportunities and resources, girls in the developing world are generally disadvantaged compared to boys. This disadvantage is especially acute among girls who are married at very young ages. Young married girls are least likely to benefit from educational and economic policies and programs, such as those that encourage primary and secondary school enrollment or expand opportunities for credit or participation in the paid workforce. Indeed, many of the basic resources and services available to other segments of the population are beyond the reach of young married girls.

Early marriage sharply reduces girls' access to education, while anticipation of early marriage often precludes education (Huq and Amin 2001). Furthermore, since in most cultures girls leave their parental home upon marriage, parents are often less interested in investing in the education of daughters (as opposed to sons) because the benefits of their investment will be lost. After marriage, young married girls' access to formal and even non-formal education is severely limited because of a lack of mobility, domestic burdens, childbearing, and social norms that view marriage and schooling as incompatible. Data shows that girls with fewer than seven years of schooling are more likely to be married by age 18 than those with higher levels of schooling.

Similarly, the enrollment of young women in secondary school is inversely related to the proportion of girls married before the age of 18. Early marriage, early childbearing, and lack of access to continued educational opportunities limit young women's access to employment opportunities and, in turn, their productive value to society. Young women's employment is often seen as a threat to culturally accepted gender roles, and many families fear for the safety of girls at workplaces. Moreover, even when young married girls want to work or need to earn money in order to support their families, they have few marketable skills that can translate into high-paying jobs or entrepreneurial options.

This does not mean, however, that young married girls do not work. In fact, research shows that the majority of young married girls are either employed in home-based work or the informal sector (Population Council and ICRW 2000). Informal work is characterized by parttime or casual jobs that do not have the benefits and security of regular employment and that are performed outside the scope or application of legal and institutional frameworks (Farnsworth Riche 2003). At home, young married women are primarily responsible for household-related tasks, yet they have limited access to productive resources such as land, housing, credit, water, and agricultural technical assistance (Panda 2002).

As young brides, girls are virtually entrapped at home as "apprentices" in charge of domestic responsibilities. As a result, their social mobility is dramatically reduced (Mensch, Bruce, and Greene 1998). Nor have they experienced a period during adolescence in which they could interact with their peers and develop friendships and social support systems. Research in Nepal shows that young girls in general lack safe social spaces, and that those who are married are particularly isolated from peers (Mathur et al. 2001).

LACK OF POWER

Since early marriage limits skills, resources, knowledge, social support, mobility, and autonomy, young married girls often have little power in relation to their husbands or in-laws. They are also extremely vulnerable to violence, abuse, divorce, and abandonment. Violence may include physical, sexual, psychological, and economic abuse. Data from Chile, Peru, Malaysia, Mexico, Panama, Papua New Guinea, and the United States shows that between one-third and two-thirds of known sexual assault victims are 15 years old or younger (Heise, Pitanguy, and Germain 1994). In Haiti, for example, 25 percent of young, married women aged 15-19 have experienced violence within marriage in the last year.

Young women's initiation into sexual activity often occurs under coercive conditions. Thus, even within unions that are formally consensual, nonconsensual sexual activity is common (Heise, Ellsberg, and Gottemoeller 1999). This is particularly the case when girls are economically dependent on their husbands, and are thereby not in a position to resist violence or coercion or to negotiate condom use or other preferences. A study of women's risk for HIV/ AIDS in 15 countries found that women frequently mentioned being physically forced to have sex or to engage in types of sexual activity that they found degrading and humiliating (Weiss and Gupta 1998). Many other women stated that they gave in to sex out of fear of the consequences of refusal, such as physical abuse, loss of economic support, or accusations of infidelity.

Outcomes for Children

The consequences of early marriage reach beyond the lives of young married girls themselves to the next generation. Poor infant and child health outcomes are strongly associated with the early age of mothers, due in part to young women's physical vulnerabilities and in part to the lack of social and reproductive health services for this high-risk group. In most countries, infants and children of mothers who give birth to them before the age of 20 face consistently higher mortality rates even through the age of five.10 The starkest effects are seen in the Infant Mortality Rate (IMR), which is 181 per 1,000 for the children women in Mali who give birth before age 20, versus 111 per 1,000 for the children of women who give birth at age 20-29. The corresponding figures are 164 versus 88 in Tanzania, 108 versus 68 in Nepal, and 71 versus 28 in the Dominican Republic.

Development Outcomes

Early marriage stands in direct conflict with the objectives of the Millennium Development Goals (MDGs), such as the promotion of basic education, child survival, and the prevention of HIV/ AIDS.11 When the relationship between age at marriage and development is examined, it becomes clear that later marriage is a precondition for the attainment of desired developmentrelated goals. These can include completion of school, acquisition of training for employment, and attainment of the skills and information related to the roles of citizen, family member, and consumer that are part of a successful adulthood. The link between age at marriage and development holds at the societal level as well.

Thus, when the relationship between early marriage and the Human Development Index (HDI) indicators is examined, the negative relationship between widespread early marriage and national development is quite striking. Countries where the proportion of currently married 15-19-year-old women is high have a low rank on the HDI. Many factors affect both early marriage and human development, but reducing the former is certainly an important part of the equation for attaining successful national development.

PROGRAMMATIC AND POLICY RESPONSES TO EARLY MARRIAGE

In many cultures, early marriage for girls is strongly entrenched. However, social and economic investment and active policy and programmatic efforts can bring about changes in social norms and institutions that will lead to later marriage for young girls. Improvements in social welfare, employment, and education levels have been associated with later age at marriage for women in countries such as the Republic of Korea, Sri Lanka, Taiwan, and Thailand (Xenos and Kabamalan 1998 and Malhotra and

Tsui 1996). In other settings, policies aimed at changing laws, regulations, social norms, attitudes, and opportunities related to girls have yielded positive results. Some initiatives have also reduced the negative effects of early marriage for young married girls. Examples follow of successful efforts to meet the following goals using a range of strategies.

Goal: Delay Marriage

By Providing Economic Opportunities

Research in Bangladesh and Taiwan shows that when jobs are available to girls, both daughters and parents become interested in delaying marriage. The garment industry in Bangladesh has played an important role in extending the period before marriage, while at the same time providing young women with the means to earn a living (Amin et al. 1998).

- A number of Indian states have developed long-term programs that allow young women to receive the money that the state invested in them at birth only when they have completed a certain level of schooling and are still unmarried (Government of Manipur 1997).

By Educating Girls

- The acceptance of education as a desirable activity for girls during their adolescent years has been a critical factor in increasing age at marriage in a number of Asian countries, including Indonesia, Taiwan, Thailand, and Sri Lanka. In India and Pakistan as well, increased school enrollment has been associated with a decline in marriage among girls before age 14 (Hussain and Bittles 1999 and Unisa 1995).
- In Bangladesh, secondary school scholarships for girls have had an immediate effect in delaying marriage

(Arends-Kuenning 2000 and Amin and Gilda 1998). Both girls and their parents receive a stipend that is conditional upon the girl remaining unmarried through completion of the 10th standard. In areas targeted by the project, female enrollment in secondary schooling more than doubled between 1994 and 2001 (World Bank Group 2003).

- The state of Gujarat in India has offered new bicycles to girls completing the 10th standard, an approach that effectively provides both education and mobility (Greene 1997).

Source: Population Reference Bureau 2000; United Nations Development Programme 2002

By Creating Safe Social Spaces

- Parents need to be reassured that when their unmarried daughters leave the house, they will be in safe places and can get to where they are going without harm. This concern is an important reason why girls experience reduced mobility and early marriage. A program in Kenya has allowed girls to play soccer together, providing them with opportunities to be with peers and to be exposed to health messages and other information provided by adult mentors (Brady and Khan 2002). In this way, a safe social space becomes an alternative to early marriage.

- The Ghanaian government has just launched a major campaign creating "Sara Clubs" for girls who encourage each other to stay in school. Some of the major themes addressed in this campaign and through club activities include early marriage, sexual exploitation, HIV/AIDS, and unwanted pregnancy (UNICEF and JHUCCP 2003).

Through Public Education and Enforcement of Existing Laws and Regulations

- Women's groups in a number of countries are trying to hold governments accountable for prosecuting individuals who force young women to marry their rapists.
- The state of Uttar Pradesh in India has worked to increase awareness of the legal minimum age at marriage (18 years) and to deny government jobs to people who marry before that age (Government of Uttar Pradesh 2000).
- A district-level campaign in Rajasthan, India, has prolonged the traditional period of engagement, allowing girls to marry a little later (Chandrasekhar 1996).
- Educating parents and other community members about the harm caused by early marriage is increasingly recognized as an important undertaking. The Government of Nepal, in collaboration with the United Nations Fund for Population Activities (UNFPA), has created educational materials that encourage parents to delay marrying their daughters until they are over the age of 20 (Nepal Health Education, Information, and Communication Center 1995).

Goal: Address the Needs of Married Youth

By Preparing Young People for the Challenges of Sexual Relationships

Increasingly, programs are being developed and implemented in recognition of the need to provide young people with access to reproductive health information and services both before and after marriage. Since all young people are "atrisk" of early marriage, providing them with the right tools for safe sexual and reproductive lives is immensely important.13

- In Nepal and India, international and incountry groups operate adolescent reproductive health programs that provide information and services to married and unmarried adolescent boys and girls. Young people receive information on a range of issues, including puberty, sexual intercourse, and childbearing. In addition, program staff work with health providers and members of the community to make reproductive health services and counseling more accessible to young people.
- In Botswana, Ghana, Tanzania, and Uganda, adolescent reproductive health programs collaborate with health service providers in order to make services more friendly and accessible to young people. Programs also focus on providing life skills and reproductive health information so that both married and unmarried young people can learn how to avoid disease and unwanted pregnancies.

By Providing Negotiation Skills for Sexual Relationships

Program strategies have focused on developing curricula that impart life skills information to young people, which is particularly important because young girls are vulnerable to coercion, sexual abuse, and violence even within marriage. Some programmatic efforts have focused on developing girls' ability to negotiate sexual relations within marriage (Brown 2001).

- Program staff in Mexico, South Africa, and Thailand are implementing a school-based HIV/AIDS curriculum for both young women and men that places special emphasis on life skills (Stewart et al. 2001).

- In India, married and unmarried girls are provided with life skills training to help them prepare and navigate their sexual and reproductive lives before and within marriage (Esim et al. 2001).

By Focusing on the Needs of Couples

Some countries are creatively using marriage registration systems to provide young people with reproductive health information.

- Iran has made reproductive health counseling a prerequisite for obtaining a marriage license (Greene et al. 2002).
- In Indonesia, marriage counselors from the Islamic marriage registry system have been trained as reproductive health educators (Dornsife and Mahmoed 1985).
- Mexico's National Population Council has assisted three states in requiring a statement from a doctor or social worker indicating that a couple has discussed reproductive health matters before a marriage license can be obtained (UNFPA 1990).

Some governments and NGOs make an effort to specifically reach young married couples through their services, clinics, and programs.

- As part of a large intervention research program in India, several NGOs have tested innovative models to improve services for young married couples by working with the couples themselves, communities, and health providers (ICRW 2001).
- In China and Bangladesh, family planning workers visit young couples who have recently had a child with congratulatory letters that also encourage them to take advantage of existing family planning services (Alauddin and Rob 1999).

- In many countries, health workers are being trained to show more sensitivity toward young people, especially married couples (Alauddin and Rob 1999).
- In northern India, groups such as the Foundation for Research in Health Systems and the Society for the Integrated Development of the Himalayas are working with young married girls and their husbands to explore constraints and identify the best approaches for increasing access to and utilization of health services by young married couples (Gupta, Joshi, and Crook 2003 and Barua et al. 2003).

Goal: Improve Education and Economic Options for Young Married Women

- Efforts to improve the access of young married girls to economic resources have focused on expanding employment and entrepreneurial opportunities. Additional efforts to enforce property and inheritance laws and to mobilize community efforts may also be required.
- Several well-known economic and livelihood programs, such as the Grameen Bank in Bangladesh and the Self-Employed Women's Association in India, have begun to include young married girls in their initiatives.
- In an effort to continue girls' schooling after marriage, Iran has established a few schools specifically for young married women (Greene et al. 2002).
- In Kenya, local groups have organized nonformal education and livelihood training sessions for teen mothers.

CONCLUSION

Despite international agreements and national laws to the contrary, the practice of marrying girls below the age of 18 is prevalent in many parts of the world and affects the lives of millions of young girls. As a result, girls-even when they are still children-often are defined solely as wives and mothers and are exposed to responsibilities and risks for which they are often not physically or mentally prepared. When married young, girls lose the opportunities for education, employment, or other important experiences for the duration of their lives. The negative developmental consequences that early marriage has in the realms of health, welfare, and economics not only affect girls and their children, but also societies as a whole.

In many countries, a combination of tradition, poverty, and lack of opportunity put a large number of young people "at-risk" for early marriage. Increased policy and program attention toward young people is therefore critically needed and warranted. Although early marriage remains a pervasive practice, there is evidence that social and economic investments can make a significant difference in improving the life options of young people. Fortunately, many governments, NGOs, and development agencies are recognizing the need-often as part of overall efforts to improve development outcomes-to address the problem of early marriage through a range of policy and programmatic solutions.

These efforts are targeted both at delaying marriage and at equipping those who are married young with increased access to the information, resources, skills, and services they need to deal with their situation. It is clear that programmatic and policy actions need to address not only the legal basis of early marriage, but also its social and economic underpinnings. Continued effort should be made to understand the needs of girls and their families, as well as the types of innovative, targeted strategies that can effectively counter the practice of early marriage.

5

ENDING CHILD MARRIAGE

A Guide for Global Policy Action appeals to key policy makers to improve the quality of life of millions of girls and young women forced into child marriages. Globally, vulnerable and marginalized rural girls and women continue to bear the health risks and social and economic costs of early and forced marriage, non-consensual sex and early pregnancies. There is now greater urgency for global policy action because child brides are increasingly more vulnerable to HIV infection.

The persistent neglect of the plight of child brides in parts of South Asia, Africa, the Middle East and Latin America is a direct reflection of the failure of our collective responsibility to protect the human rights of vulnerable young people.

The silenced voices of the many millions of young women and girls forced into marriage before their eighteenth birthday signify complacency and discrimination. Most countries have laws on the minimum age of marriage, but they are largely ineffective, not enforced or operate alongside customary and religious laws. Traditions and cultural norms which rule the social lives of many practising communities in the developing world should not be used as an excuse to neglect the duty to protect, respect and fulfil the rights of young women.

Ending child marriage is indeed a mandatory task if we are to make progress in global efforts to attain the Millennium Development Goals (MDGs). It is that simple. But this will require unambiguous political commitment, visionary leadership, and support for grassroots advocacy to address many of the cultural practices and behaviours that place young women and girls at increased multiple health risks, including HIV.

Ending Child Marriage: A Guide for Global Policy Action makes a strong case for international action, and strengthens the advocacy efforts of development practitioners and women's and children's rights activists to end child marriage. This work is a result of a series of technical consultations on child marriage, organized by the International Planned Parenthood Federation (IPPF) in collaboration with the Forum on Marriage and the Rights of Women and Girls. This practical tool documents the special needs of child brides and outlines the nature of the economic and social factors which reinforce the practice.

It provides solutions based on a child protection framework, and advocates for the use of legal, policy and multi-sector programme strategies for delaying child marriage for those at risk and meeting the needs of young women who are newly married.

It will add value to other ongoing efforts to end child marriage and promote the rights and true voices of countless young people, in particular girls and young women around the globe, who have been marginalized for far too long.

IPPF's mission includes a commitment to "defend the rights of all young people to enjoy their sexual lives free from ill health, unwanted pregnancy, violence and discrimination." We will continue to collaborate and advocate for an enabling policy environment to bring an end to child marriage.

This advocacy tool is also part of the wider initiative on preventing HIV infection, particularly among adolescent girls, which is led by the United Nations Global Coalition on Women and AIDS (GCWA), with the support of the United Nations Population Fund (UNFPA) and Young Positives. Collectively, we have the power to change the course of this epidemic and bring dignity and empowerment to women and girls. We believe that bold policy decision making that takes into account the special concerns of child brides in national and international policy and programme responses will help us today to transform the lives of tomorrow's generation.

The development of this work was made possible through the support and guidance of members of the Forum on Marriage and the Rights of Women and Girls. In particular, Ingrid Lewis, Maggie Black, Adwoa Kwateng Kluvitse, Edward Wageni and Romana Cacchioli, who helped to write and shape different parts of this publication, provided case studies and reviewed the numerous versions.

The recommendations in this publication represent the voices of several organizations and participants who attended two technical consultations organized jointly by IPPF and the Forum on Marriage and the Rights of Women and Girls. We are grateful for their expertise and enthusiasm. They include those who took part in the Technical Consultation on Child Marriage (Nairobi, Kenya, October 2005) and in the Ouagadougou Technical Consultation on Early and Forced Marriage and the Rights of Women and Girls (October 2003).

We are especially grateful to other individuals who freely offered their time and expertise to review and guide this work, namely Jaya Sagade, Elisabeth Paulson, Boatema Boateng and Naomi Namugenyi. In IPPF, Naana Otoo-Oyortey led on this initiative with the support of the members of the Technical Knowledge and Support Division, in particular Kevin Osborne, Tim Shand, Andy Guise and Upeka de Silva. Additional support was provided by the Communication Team, Karla Fitzhugh and Chris Wells. Finally we are grateful to the Director of the Technical Knowledge and Support Division, Princess Nono Simelela, who provided invaluable support and guidance.

THE REALITY OF CHILD BRIDES

"I am one of those unfortunate Hindu women whose hard lot is to suffer the unnameable miseries entailed by the custom of early marriage. This wicked practice of child marriage has destroyed the happiness of my life. It comes between me and the thing which I prize above all others-study and mental cultivation. Without the least fault of mine I am doomed to seclusion; every aspiration of mine to rise above my ignorant sisters is looked upon with suspicion and is interpreted in the most uncharitable manner." Rukhambai, Letter to the Times of India, 26 June 1885

"You are becoming an obstacle to opportunity of the girls who have been asked for marriage. The government does not give them jobs. What will happen to them? Do you want them to go to the cities?"

A response from an elder during field interviews, Ethiopia 2005 "In Niger, which has the highest proportion of girls aged 15-19 currently in union (60 per cent), a girl in union is most likely to live in a rural area (91 per cent), to have received no education (90 per cent) and to be disproportionately located in the second wealth quintile (33 per cent). She is unlikely to have co-wives (79 per cent), and if she has children (43 per cent have no children) she is likely to have only one or two (56 per cent). Her husband is more likely to be 5-9 years older than she is (38 per cent) compared to other age gaps considered, and it is likely that neither partner received an education (73 per cent). She is likely to know how to protect herself from HIV/AIDS (64 per cent) but is unlikely to have ever used any form of contraception (89 per cent)." UNICEF, 2005

WHY IS CHILD MARRIAGE A GLOBAL CONCERN?

Today, the devastating impact of child marriage continues to be ignored in the developing world. Millions of child brides, some only just past puberty, are denied access to health, education and economic opportunities. The majority of them are burdened with the roles and responsibilities of wives and mothers without adequate support, resources or capabilities. This is despite the existence of numerous international and regional human rights laws and conventions against the practice.

It is clear that international human rights instruments relating to child marriage remain, at best, rhetoric, or general declarations of principles, without effective national policies and mechanisms to implement and enforce them.

There is now an urgent need to do things differently, if the international development agendas agreed by governments within the last decade, particularly the International Conference on Population and Development (ICPD), the Fourth World Conference on Women, and more recently the Millennium Development Goals are to become a reality.

Child marriage remains a widely ignored violation of the health and development rights of girls and young women. Governments are often either unable to enforce existing laws, or rectify discrepancies between national laws on marriage age and entrenched customary and religious laws. This is because of the "official tolerance of cultural, societal and customary norms that shape and govern the institution of marriage and family life."

In general, there is seldom political will to act when it comes to women's and girls' human rights. Additionally, the international development community has largely failed to target development assistance to address this gross rights violation. Child marriage is culturally packaged as a social necessity, but in many cases this amounts to "socially licensed sexual abuse and exploitation of a child."

It is one of the most persistent forms of sanctioned sexual abuse of girls and young women. "The fact that the arrangement is socially accepted does not diminish the reality that a girl is deliberately exposed to sexual abuse and exploitation, usually by her parents and family." The silence on the plight of child brides must end, particularly because of the increasing evidence that child marriage is a risk factor for HIV infection. The young age of child brides, their limited power in sexual decision making and reduced economic opportunities compound their vulnerability to multiple health risks.

Many valid reasons are given by parents and guardians to justify child marriage. Economic reasons often underpin these decisions which are directly linked to poverty and the lack of economic opportunities for girls in rural areas. Girls are either seen as an economic burden or valued as capital for their exchange value in terms of goods, money or livestock.

A combination of cultural, traditional and religious arguments also justifies child marriage. The fear and stigma attached to premarital sex and bearing children outside marriage, and the associated family honour, are often seen as valid reasons for the actions that families take. Finally, many parents tend to curtail the education of their girls and marry them off, due to fear of the high level of sexual violence and abuse encountered en route to, and even at, school. Tackling child marriage is a daunting but possible task, requiring political will and proactive multi-faceted strategies at the international, national and community levels.

Ending Child Marriage: A Guide for Global Policy Action is part of a wider advocacy strategy to raise awareness on child marriage and its effects on communities. It aims to stimulate decision makers worldwide-in particular government policy makers, donors, and international development agencies-to take all necessary measures to end this violation of rights. The publication outlines this global problem and the reasons why child marriage persists, assesses how it contravenes many international human rights standards, and then provides policy and programmatic recommendations. It will assist organizations to accelerate action and advocate for an end to this practice.

What is Child Marriage?

Child marriage, also known as early marriage, is defined as "[A]ny marriage carried out below the age of 18 years, before the girl is physically, physiologically, and psychologically ready to shoulder the responsibilities of marriage and childbearing." Marriage is a formalized, binding partnership between consenting adults, which sanctions sexual relations and gives legitimacy to any offspring. It is still a respected and valued social institution throughout the world, and may take different forms in different cultures.

Child marriage, on the other hand, involves either one or both spouses being children and may take place with or without formal registration, and under civil, religious or customary laws. In many societies in developing countries, child marriages are used to build or strengthen alliances between families. Sometimes this may even include the betrothals of young children or babies. The 1948 Universal Declaration of Human Rights states that marriage should be "entered only with the free and full consent of the intending spouses." But, in the majority of child marriages, there is often an element of coercion involved:

parents, guardians or families pressurize, collude or force children into marriage. Today girls are still socialized into accepting child marriage as the norm, a 'given', and many give their consent as a duty and sign of respect. However, where one of the parties in a marriage is under 18 years, consent to marry in such cases cannot always be assumed to be of 'free and full consent' and may also not always be in the best interest of the child.

The UN Convention on the Rights of the Child (CRC) defines a child as "every human being below the age of eighteen years unless, under the law applicable to the child, majority is attained earlier." The expert body that monitors the Convention on the Elimination on All Forms of Discrimination against Women (CEDAW) in its General Recommendation 21, which explicitly deals with equality in marriage and family relations, outlaws child marriage, and stipulates 18 years as the minimum age for marriage for males and females. This is the minimum age when young people attain "full maturity and capacity to act."

This acknowledges that, from a child rights and equity perspective, marriage should not be permissible before 18 years of age. Although an adolescent girl may attain sexual maturity early, she will often not be physically mature enough to conceive a child, nor will she be cognitively or psychologically mature enough for marriage and the related responsibilities of being a wife and mother.

A new study by UNICEF-Early Marriage: A Harmful Traditional Practice: A Statistical Exploration-argues that young women in informal unions are equally as vulnerable as child brides. Cohabitation creates similar human rights concerns as marriage and young women under 18 years in such unions live with partners and take on similar roles as care givers, wives and mothers. However, the informal nature of these unions means that they are neither protected by customary nor by civil laws. Informal unions are more common in parts of Latin America, and may present equally challenging and adverse consequences for affected young women. Also "the informality of the relationship-for example, inheritance, citizenship and social recognition-might make girls in informal unions vulnerable in different ways than those in formally recognized marriages."

Some of the data used in this publication may not differentiate between children involved in formal or informal unions, since many of the health and social consequences related to child brides aged below 18 apply equally to cohabitating young women.

A GLOBAL SNAPSHOT OF THE PROBLEM AND ITS IMPACT

Traditional notions of child marriage continue to justify it as a positive social norm with social and financial benefits.

However, new studies on the health and social consequences reveal far more damaging results. Child marriage is a public health concern that violates international human rights laws and seriously compromises the development and health of affected individuals. Child brides are pressured to initiate sexual activity and become mothers too early. The consequences of child marriage are often far wider than just their impact on the individual children affected. The marriage of children has negative effects on families and communities. The practice thrives on poverty and impacts adversely on a country's health and education sectors. Yet everywhere child brides and child mothers are overlooked and invisible in national policy and programme debates, despite their unique situation and vulnerability.

Trends in the Practice of Child Marriage

It is very difficult to get accurate data on the true extent of child marriages. This is because most marriages are not officially registered, and many parents resort to falsifying girls' ages. Such acts are made easier in rural areas where birth certificates are often non-existent or not properly recorded. There is also very little data on girls married before the age of 15. Available data are often outdated and fail to provide adequate information to support meaningful policy and programme development. But research and policy action has continued to focus mainly on the concerns of unmarried young people. Although child marriage is said to be declining in many parts of the world, the total number of girls at risk or affected is very significant and cannot be ignored. It was estimated in 2004 that, within the next decade, more than 100 million girls in the developing world would be married before the age of 18.10

The UNICEF statistical study on child marriage confirms that the practice is most common in South Asia, where over 48 per cent of 15–24-year-olds were married before they reached 18. In Africa this figure is 42 per cent (though this rises to over 60 per cent in parts of East and West Africa), and in Latin America and the Caribbean the figure is 29 per cent. In the Middle East, child marriage is common in Yemen and Palestine, and here about half of under-18s were already married.

Statistics on the prevalence of child marriage reveal sectors or areas of countries – such as ethnic, religious or socio-economic groups – where a large majority of adolescent girls are married before their fifteenth birthday.12 Table 1 provides data on such marriage 'hotspots' within selected countries in West Africa, South Asia and Latin America. Within large countries, such as India and Nigeria, there are often significant disparities in numbers of child marriages across states and regions. Additionally, among conflict or disaster-affected populations, rates of child marriage tend to increase as parents in distress seek to secure girls' sexual protection or to increase economic survival through marriage. Child marriage – in particular marriages of under-15s – is more common in rural communities.

This is because rural households tend to have more entrenched traditional attitudes and customs, are less affected by external influences, and have fewer livelihood options for young women. In general, child marriage is more prevalent among poorer families, although where the practice is virtually universal it may be almost as common among wealthier families. Marriage of girls often correlates with low levels of education, or no education. The UNICEF statistical study, which is the most comprehensive global analysis on child marriage, found that in 47 countries girls aged 15–19 who had higher levels of education were least likely to be in any marriage union. Only in a small number of countries were girls with secondary education equally likely to be married.13

Globally, child marriage affects more girls than boys: on average only 5 per cent of males marry before they reach 19 years. Even though child marriage is predominantly a problem of developing countries, there is still evidence of the practice in a few developed countries, including the United States where parents can give consent to the marriage of their daughters below the age of 15 years.

Health Costs of Early Sexual Initiation and Early Pregnancy

"For every woman who dies in childbirth, some 15 to 30 survive but suffer chronic disabilities, the most devastating of which is obstetric fistula. Fistula is an injury to a woman's birth canal that leaves her leaking urine and/or faeces. Young women under age 20 are especially prone to developing fistulas if they cannot get a Caesarean section during prolonged obstructed labour. Prevalence is highest in impoverished communities in Africa and Asia." (UNFPA, 2003)

Child marriage is often associated with multiple health risks. This is because young brides have limited access to, and use of, contraception and reproductive health services and information. The majority are exposed to early and frequent sexual relations and to repeated pregnancies and childbirth before they are physically mature and psychologically ready. Obstetric fistula is one of the most devastating consequences, with over two million girls and young women affected by this treatable and indeed preventable reproductive health complication. Pregnancy-related deaths are also the leading cause of mortality in 15–19-year-old girls, and those aged under 15 years are five times more likely to die than those aged over 20. Infant deaths are also twice as high in babies of very young mothers.16 A study in Niger confirmed that pregnant young women from poorer communities are eight times less likely to deliver with the assistance of a skilled birth attendant than young women from the wealthiest quintile of their community.

A study on contraceptive use among 15–19-year-old girls in unions found that many felt pressurized by families to prove their fertility very early in the marriage. For example, 46 per cent of girls in unions had never used any contraception, and only 31 per cent stated that they used modern contraceptive methods.18

Child brides are also least likely to use reproductive services because of their limited decision making powers and economic dependency. Many married girls either do not know about contraception or are unable to negotiate its use due to fear of violence from their spouses, who often tend to be older. A World Health Organization multi-country study on women's health and domestic violence found that age was a key risk factor. Younger women, particularly those aged 15–19, with lower levels of education had a higher risk of physical or sexual violence perpetrated by a partner in all the study countries except Japan and Ethiopia. "In urban Bangladesh, 48 per cent of 15–19-year-old women reported either physical or sexual violence, or both, by a partner within the past 12 months, versus 10 per cent of 45–49-year-olds. In urban Peru, the difference was 41 per cent among 15–19-year-olds versus 8 per cent of 45–49-year-olds."

Domestic violence thrives in an environment where women feel powerless and lack access to vital resources and decision making powers. Child marriages tend to create a multitude of conditions that make affected young women vulnerable to violence. The wide age gap between child brides and their spouses makes them less able to negotiate, they have limited social support networks, are economically dependent and have limited mobility. Younger child brides may also be at risk of sexual violence and abuse from older men in their spouses' families, and are known to be more likely to tolerate violence and less likely to leave abusive partners.

Increased Vulnerability to HIV

"These data call into question the often deeply ingrained belief that marriage protects young women from HIV. First, for many adolescents – particularly the youngest brides – marriage greatly increases their potential exposure to the virus, because marriage results in a transition from virginity to frequent unprotected sex."

Despite recent gains in expanding access to HIV prevention and treatment, the epidemic is worsening among young women. The general belief (even among policy makers and communities) that marriage protects girls from HIV infection effectively condones the practice of child marriage. However, recent research conducted by the Population Council shows that child wives are more vulnerable to contracting HIV, particularly in generalized epidemics. Contributory factors include the young age at marriage, the wide spousal age gap, frequency of unprotected sexual activity, limited access to information and negotiation powers.

Marriage often increases sexual activity and the likelihood of exposure and risk, particularly because many young brides cannot negotiate safe sex (even when they have knowledge about how to protect themselves) and are under pressure to demonstrate their fertility. It would both be negligent and discriminatory against child brides if their vulnerability to HIV, particularly in parts of sub-Saharan Africa, is not recognized and addressed.

Table : Percentage of young women aged 15–24 married by age 15, married by age 18, and infected with HIV, by country and regional hotspot

Country (regional hotspot)	% married by age 15		% married by age 18		Nationwide HIV prevalence rate in young women aged 15–24
	Nation-wide	Regional hotspot	Nation-wide	Regional hotspot	
Ethiopia (Amhara)	19	50	49	80	10.0
Mozambique (Nampula)	22	53	57	82	18.8
Nigeria (Northwest)	19	41	43	79	7.0
Tanzania (Shinyinga)	6	14	39	59	9.7
Uganda (Eastern)	15	21	54	63	5.6
Zambia (Luapula)	9	16	44	55	25.2

Source: Population Council (2005) cited from Demographic and Health Surveys and UNAIDS

Traditional HIV prevention strategies have focused on the 'ABC' approach: abstinence, being faithful and relying on condoms. The reality is that "many of the world's women are simply not in a position to abstain from sex, rely on fidelity or negotiate condom use. ABC can only be a viable and effective prevention option for women and girls if it is implemented as part of a multi-faceted package of interventions that seek to redress deep-rooted gender imbalances."

A publication on HIV and young people revealed in a study in Pune, India, that a quarter of women in an antenatal clinic had contracted a sexually transmitted infection (STI) and about 14 per cent were already HIV positive. The majority were married and 91 per cent reported they had only had sexual relations with their husbands. UNAIDS data show that 60 per cent of new HIV infections in Africa alone are among young women aged 15–24, and in parts of Africa and the Caribbean young women are nearly six times more likely to be infected with HIV than young men. This means that young women are engaging in unprotected sex and are either unable to access relevant information or have little power to protect themselves.

The UN Task Force on Women, Girls and HIV/AIDS in southern Africa identified three key factors that fuel the vulnerability of women and girls to HIV infection. The general culture of silence around sexuality, exploitative transactional and intergenerational sex, and violence against women. These factors in conjunction with the wider root causes of poverty and gender inequalities make women and girls vulnerable to HIV. This is further worsened by myths that drive men to marry virgins in the hope of being 'cured' of HIV. Traditions such as widow cleansing in some parts of Africa and Asia require widows to have sexual relations with total strangers or relatives. In other cultures widows are forced to marry a dead husband's brother. Child brides will invariably be more likely to go along with many of these traditional norms and social pressures.

The global HIV pandemic is now recognized as requiring exceptional responses, and a new way forward is to acknowledge that many HIV prevention programmes have failed to reach out to vulnerable young women. Without redressing entrenched gender norms and codes of conduct on sexual relationships, gender discrimination and inequalities will further increase young women's vulnerability. In addition, child brides who are HIV positive will become more marginalized and less able to access much needed treatment and care.

EDUCATION AND DEVELOPMENT OPPORTUNITY COSTS

"Immediately after we were withdrawn from the school by our father, my maternal uncle came to ask for our hands in marriage for his sons. My sister and I refused. Our father forced us and of course we were married against our will and this was the first injustice done to us. I was 13 years old and I had just started menstruating. I was engaged for a year before I was married off at 14 years of age. I became pregnant three months after I got married." A 19-year-old girl from Yemen, in conversation with Dr Husnia Al-Kadri and Maha El-Metwally26 Education and social development are key areas where many child brides lose out when they are married too early. In large parts of Asia, Africa and in some Middle Eastern communities, girls are not enrolled in school or are withdrawn at puberty, often to undertake domestic duties or specifically for marriage.

Education and employment outside the home may be considered irrelevant or undesirable where women's roles are confined to those of daughter, wife and mother. This is more so for girls from poor communities who have less access to education, and are more likely to marry early. Several studies confirm a strong correlation between the level of women's education and their use of reproductive health services. Secondary education, in particular, improves women's status, delays the age of marriage, and enhances reproductive decision making. Conversely, women who are poor and have little education "tend to start childbearing at younger ages, have more children too close together, and prolong childbearing."

The children of young, uneducated mothers are also less likely to attain high levels of education, perpetuating cycles of low literacy and limited livelihood opportunities. Child marriage deprives societies of the intellectual and financial/livelihood contributions of girls, and of their offspring. Human rights research shows that the greatest obstacles to girls' education – as identified in many government reports to human rights monitoring bodies – are child marriage, pregnancy and domestic chores.

The curtailment of girls' education in this way directly undermines national and international efforts to achieve targets on education and gender equality in education. Reduced literacy levels ultimately lead to a reduction in employment or income generation options, and impair the ability of child wives to absorb and utilize information. This tends to affect autonomy in making key decisions, including those that relate to their reproductive health and the well-being of their children. Girls who are denied education are also invariably denied exposure outside the home environment, resulting in low self-confidence, further perpetuating women's powerlessness and vulnerability to poverty.

The current international development targets, the MDGs, particularly those on poverty, universal primary education, maternal and child mortality, and HIV/AIDS, have not been met in many countries in Africa. Child marriage directly hampers efforts to achieve the MDGs, as the box on the next page illustrates.

When girls' education is disrupted to get them married early, they also lose valued opportunities to other benefits of formal education. This makes the smooth transition from adolescence into adulthood for the majority of married girls very problematic. Where the transition to adulthood is managed and supported, the majority of young women and girls become more empowered to effectively play their future roles as women, mothers, wives, wage earners and active citizens of their country. Education is known to play a vital part in this transition. Yet "girls of primary school age not only are precluded from school but also lose their rights as children. Child marriage transforms a school girl into an adult, even if she is only seven years old."

Child marriage impedes the Millennium Development Goals30 Ending child marriage will have a direct effect on realizing six of the MDGs, the key development priorities until 2015, agreed by governments and the international community in September 2000.

Goal 1: Eradicate extreme poverty and hunger. Child mothers often have limited skills, education and access to the economic assets and decision making powers necessary to properly nourish their offspring, and are therefore likely to perpetuate the cycle of poverty.

Goal 2: Achieve universal primary education. Access to universal education is a right which many girls forced into child marriage are denied. Their limited education reduces their chances of acquiring related skills and economic opportunities. Globally, there is a strong link between child marriage and low levels of education or non-education.

Goal 3: Promote gender equality and empower women. Eliminating gender inequalities and empowering young women requires access to basic capabilities such as education, health and nutrition, as well as critical social and economic resources and opportunities within an enabling environment. Child marriage disadvantages women and girls and entrenches gender inequalities.

Goal 4: Reduce child mortality. Children of child mothers are more likely to be premature and have low birth weight. Additionally, because child brides are more vulnerable to HIV, there is an increased risk that they will pass their infection to their babies. Delaying child marriage will ultimately reduce child mortality figures.

Goal 5: Improve maternal health. Maternal mortality remains a major problem for many countries in Africa which have high levels of child marriages. Child mothers have double the chance of dying during or after childbirth, and suffer more from maternal morbidities such as debilitating obstetric fistula.

Goal 6: Combat HIV/AIDS, malaria and other diseases. Marriage is a risk factor in the spread of HIV and other STIs. Child brides who marry older and more sexually experienced men have a heightened risk of contracting HIV. Reducing levels of child marriage should be an essential strategy in attaining targets for reducing the rate of HIV infection among young people aged 15–24.

Poverty, Deprivation and Risks

"Child marriage makes it harder for families, communities and countries to escape poverty. It erodes the health and well-being of girls and the overall welfare of communities. It also undercuts international efforts to fight poverty and HIV/AIDS, improve child health and survival, and support other international development initiatives, making billions of development assistance dollars less effective."

International Centre for Research on Women (2005) In many countries child marriage is linked with poverty. This is because it affects particularly the poorest in the population, and helps to reinforce cycles of poverty. Child wives tend to-have more children and fewer independent income options. But child marriages can result in the fragmentation of families, either due to early widowhood, when the older spouses of child brides die, or due to higher levels of divorce. Child brides are often more likely to experience domestic violence and least likely to take action against this abuse. The majority of affected girls become condemned to a life of financial and social insecurity. This is a real paradox for many parents, given that they marry off their daughters at a young age in the belief that this will enhance the girl's and the family's security. Poverty ultimately fuels child marriage, which in turn perpetuates the feminization of poverty.

This situation is also supported by country economic indicators for measuring the health of the economy. Several countries with very low gross domestic products (GDPs) tend to have higher rates of child marriage.

Son preference is very strong in many communities in South Asia, which may not be unrelated to the expenses involved when marrying off a daughter. The rising costs of marriage ceremonies and related dowry costs force many families to marry their daughters at the same time to reduce costs. In many villages that practise child marriage in Tamil Nadu State in India, girls are married off before they attain puberty because of the social stigma the community attaches to marriage after puberty. Many such marriages end in divorce or the girls become widows, and custom forbids divorced or widowed women to remarry, further impoverishing them.

Entrenched community norms and myths clearly help to perpetuate the practice of child marriage and related poverty. Boys forced into marriage early may also suffer financially. Economic responsibilities can place heavy burdens on them and curtail their education sooner than they might want.-However, while boys can leave their wives at their parents' homes and seek employment opportunities elsewhere, this option is not available to the majority of young wives.

Research on the link between education and poverty reduction indicates that secondary education may help reduce poverty. However, in many communities the high cost of education means that parents make choices that disrupt girls' education (marrying them off instead). This is because the majority of poor parents fail to see the "economic rationale for investing in their daughter's education." Thus national and international targets for the reduction of poverty will be harder to reach if practices like child marriage which undermine the livelihood capacities of large sections of society persist.

CHILD MARRIAGES ACROSS BORDERS

Child marriage creates numerous challenges which may be of interest at the global or regional level. In some parts of Asia, many girls are forced into child marriages to facilitate their (or their relatives') emigration to the West, particularly the UK and North America. There have been several reports of 'community marriages' in the UK, which involve underage girls marrying within immigrant communities from the Middle East, North Africa, Turkey and South Asia. Over the last decade a highly commercial form of short-term marriages has also operated in Arab countries. Here, young girls are given in marriage to wealthy men from Arab Gulf countries only to become domestic servants or abandoned after a short time period.

Many migrant girls forced into such marriages invariably encounter barriers such as language, curtailed education and limited employment opportunities in their new country. In general the majority of young women marry migrants in the hope of improving their family status. Those unable to emigrate with their husbands are often abandoned and face other economic difficulties and loss of male protection. These wives may be put under tremendous pressure to fend alone for any children that result from such temporary marriages. Child marriages linked to migration and trafficking necessitate complex relationships among authorities in the countries involved. If receiving countries have signed international commitments to uphold children's and women's rights then they will be obliged to monitor and enforce appropriate legislation to protect all child spouses who live within their borders, regardless of their place of origin.

FACTORS THAT PROMOTE AND REINFORCE CHILD MARRIAGE

Throughout the world, child marriage is held as a deeply entrenched social and economic institution, which is enshrined in religion or tradition and continues to flourish for many different reasons. The practice is similar in many ways to the social dynamics related to female genital mutilation (FGM) which is also reinforced by social norms. In several societies in Africa, child marriage is also intimately connected with FGM, because the practice forms part of the requirements of a girl for her distant or imminent marriage. As demonstrated earlier, there are a number of reinforcing factors that continue to perpetuate both practices. These pose numerous challenges for policy makers.

Family Ties

The marriage or betrothal of children in parts of Africa and Asia is valued as a means of consolidating powerful relations between families, for sealing deals over land or other property, or even for settling disputes. Marriage may also be a way of maintaining ethnic or community relations. Children's rights as individuals in such situations are often disregarded; they may instead be seen purely as commodities at the family's disposal. Betrothals are traditionally not supposed to involve sexual relations until the girl reaches adolescence, but in reality husbands are rarely restrained. Young girls may be forced or coerced to initiate sex even before it is traditionally permitted.

In parts of South Asia, the practice of families using young girls to settle family feuds is a form of child marriage, which is driven by tradition and family ties. In Pakistan, the practice of 'vani' requires giving away girls in marriage to relatives of murder victims, as compensation for crimes committed, or to settle feuds between families or clans.37

Trokosi is a form of ritual slavery practised in parts of Ghana, Togo and Benin. Girls begin their life of slavery within the shrine in pre-adolescence – some as young as four. Under this custom, a family must offer a virgin daughter to the gods to atone for the 'sins and crimes' of a relative who, in most cases, may be long dead. These crimes may range in severity from murder to petty thefts. Trokosi are always girls – literally 'wives of the gods' – forced to perform sexual services for the idol priests. Their children also become slaves of the priest, working in his fields. These girls are denied access to education and health care, and are required to spend the rest of their lives as 'wives of the gods', through the gods' medium, the fetish priest. Girls live constantly at the mercy of these fetish priests, who justify their rape and other violations with the claim that Trokosi slaves are like priestesses who copulate with the gods through their earthly servants. If a girl dies or the priest tires of her, she has to be replaced. The majority of parents are fearful of the consequences of not complying with the terms of these shrines. Anti-Slavery International, 200538

Gender Inequality

Gender inequality persists in most societies despite global statements of commitment to empower women and improve gender equality. In many societies worldwide power structures are still overwhelmingly male-dominated or patriarchal. Under such conditions, the marriage of girls is perceived as a necessary way of reinforcing existing norms. It ensures that girls and women accept their domestic roles and have a limited role within the wider society. This clearly results in women's total dependency on men. Therefore, any government making genuine efforts to eradicate gender inequality will find its path blocked unless it explicitly tackles entrenched social norms, attitudes and practices in relation to marriage, as an integral component of its gender equality strategy.

Poverty and Economic Survival Strategies

In traditional societies – where infant mortality was very high and survival depended on a family's ability to produce its own food or goods for sale – child marriage helped to maximize the number of pregnancies and ensure enough surviving children to meet household labour needs. Although the costs of raising children (e.g. funding education) may be increasingly putting pressure on families to reduce the number of births, parents in rural communities least impacted by outside influences are still motivated by traditional desires for large families. Having a large number of children, depending on the social norm, also provides a source of social security for parents in their old age.

Child marriage is valued as an economic coping strategy which reduces the costs of raising daughters. In this sense, poverty becomes a primary reason for child marriage because of perceived benefits to the family and the daughter. Marriage arrangements and requirements, such as dowry payments in parts of South Asia where parents of the young woman are obliged to give gifts to the spouse and his family, perpetuate child marriages. This is because the dowry requirement often increases with the age and the education level of the girl. Additionally, poor families tend to marry off girls at the same time to help reduce the burden of high marriage ceremony expenses.

Families in parts of sub-Saharan Africa affected by poverty and other disasters often resort to marrying off their daughters early so as to benefit from bride price or acquire additional help in the family. In some communities, men who cannot afford to pay the bride price for a woman resort to violent abduction and rape of young girls. The challenge for policy makers in such contexts is how to promote the development of alternative survival options for communities, so that child marriage and high birth rates are no longer seen as central to a family's survival.

Economic growth in many middle-level countries in North Africa and East and South East Asia has expanded opportunities for female employment within low-paid industries. This has also resulted in the erosion of many prejudices against female education and undermined the desire for child marriages. Girls instead become valued for their ability to earn income for their parents. A study in Bangladesh found that 'positive deviant' families – poor families who delayed their daughter's marriage or first birth – made their decisions primarily based on aspirations for female employment. Others felt it was justified for mature girls to stay unmarried so long as they were in school, indicating the need for more schemes to support girls' secondary education.

Control over sexuality and protecting family honour

Child marriage is traditionally recognized as necessary for controlling girls' sexuality and reproduction. Cultural and religious notions of a girl's virginity and chastity in many societies are directly linked to the honour and status of a family or clan. This means that there is tremendous pressure on parents to marry off girls early to preserve family honour and minimize the risk of improper sexual activity or conduct. Indeed, girls are perceived as incapable of protecting themselves through their own agency. Girls in rural communities may be withdrawn from school at first menstruation to restrict their movements in order to protect their sexuality. This is also linked to the belief that girls' education will, in the long term, adversely influence their future roles as wives and mothers, leading families to continue justifying child marriages.

Tradition and Culture

In communities where child marriage is prevalent there is strong social pressure on families to conform. Failure to conform can often result in ridicule, disapproval or family shame. Local myths encourage earlier marriage of girls – such as in the Amhara Region of Ethiopia where people perceive menstruation to be induced by intercourse – and such myths encourage earlier marriage of girls. Invariably, local perceptions on the ideal age for marriage, the desire for submissive wives, extended family patterns and other customary requirements (e.g. dowries or bride price), are all enshrined in local customs or religious norms. In many contexts child marriage is legitimized by patriarchy, and related family structures, which ensure that marriage transfers a father's role over his girl child to her future spouse.

This is often encouraged "to take place before a girl reaches the age when she might question it." The reality for many women and girls in rural areas is that their daily lives are more often dictated by customary laws than by national laws. Clearly, many of the social and cultural issues that reinforce child marriage indicate challenges that need to be addressed, but they also provide opportunities for advancing many development and human rights goals. The use of religion and tradition to justify child marriages shows an urgent need for developing effective strategies for collaboration with religious and traditional leaders.

Insecurity

Situations of insecurity and acute poverty, particularly during disasters such as war, famine or the HIV and AIDS epidemic, can prompt parents or carers to resort to child marriage as a protective mechanism or survival strategy. In some parts of sub-Saharan Africa the HIV and AIDS epidemic has led to an increase in child marriages. This could be due to families' desires to secure the future of their daughters. Among some populations which have been disrupted by war (e.g. in Burundi, Somalia, Northern Uganda and Afghanistan), marrying a young daughter to a warlord or someone who can look after her may be a strategy for physical security or family support. In the worst cases girls are abducted or kidnapped by armed militia or rebels and forced into temporary marriages which amount to "a combination of child prostitution and pure slavery." Displaced populations living in refugee camps may feel unable to protect their daughters from rape, and so marriage to a warlord or other authority figure may provide improved protection.

HUMAN RIGHTS OBLIGATIONS OF GOVERNMENTS

"By ratifying or acceding to international conventions, state parties accept the legal duty to abide by the conventions and thereby become obliged to take steps to protect the exercise and enjoyment of human rights, to investigate violations, and to provide effective remedies to victims." Sagade, 2005:113 One of the many benefits of being a citizen of any country is that one is entitled to a level of protection of one's rights either through the national constitution or the laws of the country.

Similarly therefore all girls and women expect their governments to protect their rights because they are citizens by law. Human rights standards and norms also require that the rights of particularly vulnerable groups be respected, protected and fulfilled. This, in practice, means that all girls should be protected from being forced into marriage at a young age. Key international and regional human rights laws on women and children have addressed in various ways the problem of child marriage.

Therefore governments have a duty to translate these laws into national legislation and introduce mechanisms to implement them. However, many countries that ratify international human rights treaties often opt out of crucial clauses relating to women's rights within marriage, and so by default endorse discrimination and gender inequality.

Why a Human Rights Framework is Critical for Stopping Child Marriage

A human rights framework provides an empowering framework for protecting vulnerable and at-risk girls from child marriage. Governments which ratify international human rights conventions are bound by minimum global standards and have a legal responsibility for preventing violations of rights. Signatory states are obliged to protect their citizens, particularly children, due to their vulnerability, dependence and specific entitlements essential for their overall development.

In the context of child marriage, although it is conducted by private individuals and not directly by the state, the state can be held responsible for "lack of diligence in preventing through its executive, legislative, or judicial organs the private act of contracting child marriage."

International human rights laws are now increasingly being used in national courts as well as in human rights treaty monitoring bodies to promote and improve girls' and women's human rights.

Key international and regional human rights instruments relating to child marriage

- *Universal Declaration of Human Rights (1948) Article 16*
- *Supplementary Convention on the Abolition of Slavery, the Slave Trade, and Institutions and Practices Similar to Slavery (1956) Article 1(c)*
- *Convention on Consent to Marriage, Minimum Age for Marriage and Registration of Marriages (1964) Articles 1, 2 and 3*
- *Convention on the Elimination of All Forms of Discrimination against Women (CEDAW) (1979) Articles 2 and 16*
- *The International Covenant on Economic, Social and Cultural Rights (1976) Article 12*
- *The Convention on the Rights of the Child (CRC) (1989) • The African Charter on the Rights and Welfare of the Child (2000) Article XXI*
- *Protocol to the African Charter on Human and People's Rights on the Rights of Women in Africa (known as the Maputo Protocol) (2003) Article 6, clauses (a), (b),(d)*

Although the international human rights conventions highlighted on the left may not provide comprehensive guidance in the area of child marriage, CEDAW – which is widely recognized as the women's bill of rights – provides explicit clauses on key areas. This includes the issue of consent, and a minimum marriage age of 18 years which outlaws discriminatory ages for males and females. The Protocol to the African Charter on Human and People's Rights on the Rights of Women in Africa (also known as the

Maputo Protocol) goes further to address all the above and calls for registration of all marriages.48 Articles 2 and 16 are-recognized as core provisions in CEDAW, addressing discrimination, marriage and family relations, but many states that have ratified this convention continue to make reservations on these key articles.

Additionally, countries which have national laws on the minimum age of marriage often do not have the political will or resources to enforce them. Nevertheless, human rights treaties monitoring bodies are beginning to take note of child marriage and can provide opportunities to hold governments accountable to child brides. A combination of international human rights conventions and national laws and policies is, essentially, the best way to make any meaningful and sustainable change on the problem of child marriage.

The Right to the Enjoyment of the Highest Attainable Standard of Physical and Mental Health

Child marriage violates the rights of girls to enjoy the highest attainable standard of physical and mental health. It is particularly in the context of sexual and reproductive health that child brides and their offspring face the greatest risks. Over 70 per cent of states in the world have ratified the International Covenant on Economic, Social and Cultural Rights, which provides standards on the right to health. Governments, therefore, have a duty to monitor compliance with this right. In particular they must ensure that information and services are made more accessible to vulnerable groups, including child mothers; are accessible to all income groups without discrimination; are acceptable to cultural needs; and are of good quality.

Three key international agreements that provide added standards for governments in realizing reproductive health and rights are the 1994 International Conference on

Population and Development; the 1995 Fourth World Conference on Women; and the 2001 and 2006 United Nations General Assembly Special Session (UNGASS) on HIV/AIDS. These landmark agreements promote human rights, gender equality and empowerment as critical to the overall development and well-being of women, girls and young women.

In the context of the HIV epidemic, governments pledged at their meeting in 2001 to progress by 2005 on a number of actions. They pledged to "ensure development and accelerated implementation of national strategies for women's empowerment, the promotion and protection of women's full enjoyment of all human rights and reduction of their vulnerability to HIV/AIDS through the elimination of all forms of discrimination, as well as forms of violence against women and girls, including harmful traditional and customary practices..."

The failure of many HIV programmes to integrate reproductive health concerns in areas of high prevalence amounts to discrimination against child brides, who are more likely to require frequent use of reproductive health services.

THE RIGHT TO EDUCATION

Several studies recognize that child marriage limits girls' rights to education. The essence of the rights to education and to health is that they facilitate and ensure the effective enjoyment of other human rights. Their denial results in the denial of other rights such as the right to work, the right to life and so on. Many child brides are withdrawn from school before they have the opportunity to acquire the relevant skills, abilities and self-confidence that will enable them to enjoy or exercise these other key human rights entitlements.

"International human rights law lays down a three-way set of criteria, whereby girls should have an equal right to education and equal rights in education, and their equal rights should be promoted through education."51 The denial of formal education means that child brides are often deprived of opportunities to access in-school programmes on HIV prevention and reproductive health information. The Convention on the Rights of the Child addresses other essential rights in relation to education.

They include the right to educational and vocational information and guidance as well as the right to seek, receive and impart information and ideas. In addition, schools are better suited to deliver the ICPD Programme of Action, including the call for programmes to meet the reproductive health needs of young people. Access to educational information and advice on reproductive health should be objective and free from stereotypes, and should support informed, full and free decision making in matters related to reproductive health and rights.52 Many child brides who become pregnant, however, are forced to leave school because of discriminatory policies and unfavourable school environments.

The Regional Charter on the Rights and Welfare of the African Child calls on parties who ratify it to ensure that child mothers complete their primary education, or are given the chance to continue their education. This clause requires enforcing the right to education for all pregnant girls and child mothers.

Often "parents, teachers and community leaders support the expulsion of pregnant girls from school, rationalizing this choice by stating the need to uphold moral norms that prohibit teenage sex, and pregnancy is treated as irrefutable proof that this norm has been breached. Adult men, including teachers, who seem to be responsible for most teenage pregnancies, have remained beyond the remit of punishment." This is a sad reality in many countries, where school discriminatory policies and gender-biased environment and limited community support systems make it impossible for married girls and young mothers to return to school.

The Right to Decide if, when and whom to Marry

A number of factors are now known to contribute to the practice of child marriage, including the state of the country's civil registration system, the lack of legislative framework and enforcement mechanisms, and the existence of traditional and religious laws that support the practice.54 An effective legal framework, which is supported by resources and enforcement mechanisms, provides a protective framework that ensures spouses' rights to decide when and whom to marry.

It also provides an enabling and supportive environment that will help to guide advocates and activists to mobilize communities to end child marriage.

CEDAW states that: "the betrothal and marriage of a child shall have no legal effect, and all necessary action, including legislation, shall be taken to specify a minimum age of marriage."

CEDAW recommends this should be 18 years for both girls and boys; an ideal age when they attain full maturity and adequate capacity to act. In reality, many laws on minimum marriage age are poorly enforced, often lack effective punitive measures or do not apply to communities in rural areas. This is because "civil, religious, customary and traditional laws often co-exist side-by-side, with no hierarchy of laws." As such many laws on minimum age of marriage are unclear, confusing and ultimately impossible to enforce. Discrimination between marriage ages for males and females is still widespread. A study in 2004 found that in 44 countries, girls were, by law, allowed to marry earlier than boys.

Article 1 of CEDAW defines 'discrimination against women' as "any distinction, exclusion or restriction made on the basis of sex which has the effect or purpose of impairing or nullifying the recognition, enjoyment or exercise by women, irrespective of their marital status, on a basis of equality of men and women, of human rights and fundamental freedoms" in all spheres. Child marriage clearly discriminates against girls because they are disproportionately affected by the practice, and bear the greater health, social and development burdens.

A key requirement of the right to marry is that all parties are able to enter marriage with their free and full consent. The right to exercise choice in relation to a spouse has also long been recognized in human rights law. But there are many serious loopholes and inconsistencies in national laws on minimum age of marriage that can undermine these rights (e.g. rapists being permitted to marry underage girls they have abused). Even where the laws are very clear, many still encourage child marriage either with parental consent or judicial authority. Where statutory laws coexist with religious and customary laws, they often fail to ensure effective protection of girls.

Clearly, many religious and customary norms lack the necessary legal clarity or do not adequately protect girls. Also, "parental consent is likewise not protective when not regulated to ensure that the principle of the best interests of the child is applied."

The Rights of the Child

Although the Convention on the Rights of the Child does not specifically address child marriage, it provides a number of norms and protective measures for children which collectively provide an enabling framework for tackling child marriage.-

While the CRC defines a child as below the age of 18 years, at the same time it allows situations where a state can legislate for this age of 18 years to be reduced. However, the articles contained in the Convention make it clear that child marriage undermines a number of rights which are guaranteed by this Convention. They include the following:

- The right to life, Article 6
- The right to health, Article 24
- The right to be protected from harmful practices, Article 24
- The right to freedom from abuse and exploitation, Articles 19, 34, 39
- The right to education, Articles 24, 28, 29
- The right to participation, Articles 12, 13, 14, 15

Remarkably, almost all countries in the world, with the exception of Somalia and the United States of America, have signed the CRC.

States Parties that sign the CRC are expected to introduce appropriate measures to ensure the implementation of the rights recognized in the Convention. Additionally the Convention stresses that in all matters concerning children, whether in the public or private arena, "the best interest of the child shall be a primary consideration."

This all confirms that child marriage falls within the protective measures outlined in the CRC, thus providing valuable opportunities to use the Convention's monitoring bodies to ensure adequate protection of girls and young women and to delay the age of marriage.

A CALL FOR GLOBAL ACTION

This policy guide has demonstrated the problem of child marriage and its impact at national and global levels. This section provides recommendations and practical steps for policy makers to respond to this problem. These actions should be viewed within the context of a wider strategy, based on action at international, national and community levels.

The challenge for governments and the international community is to demonstrate their commitment to promote and protect the rights of girls and women by introducing appropriate laws and policies. Additionally, political will is needed – in the form of resources and accountability measures – to ensure the effective implementation of laws, policies and programmes that respect rights and enhance the capacity of duty bearers, in particular parents and guardians, to meet their duties and obligations.

The recommendations provided here are based on two technical consultations on child marriage held in Burkina Faso (2003) and in Nairobi (2005). These brought together international and regional participants, from a variety of disciplines, to share research and programmes and to discuss strategies for action to address child marriage. The two consultations addressed many facets of child marriage programming and outlined priority areas of action at national, regional and international levels. These recommendations therefore reflect the views of a number of players and more recent programme lessons and can be applicable globally. This policy guide appeals to key policy makers especially governments, international development agencies, donors and non-governmental organizations to strengthen global commitments and fulfil pledges to empower women and girls by doubling efforts to end child marriages. This is a call for global action now.

Following the technical consultation on early and forced marriage held in Ouagadougou, October 2003, participants drew up a declaration, stating:

• We call on governments and international development agencies to recognize the efforts being made by civil society organizations in addressing the concerns and situation of girls and women affected by child marriages by providing the necessary support and resources to respond to the challenges posed by child and forced marriages.

• That our governments and the African Union adopt a clear and unambiguous position on child and forced marriages and rectify the legislative loopholes between religious, customary and civil marriages, and sign the Protocol to the African Charter on Human and People's Rights on the Rights of Women in Africa and ensure that special measures are taken to help end this practice.

Ouagadougou Declaration on Child Marriage, October 200360

Enact, Standardize and Enforce National Laws

National laws represent commitment by governments to translate and domesticate international human rights instruments and give guidance to policy makers and community activists. Laws should be introduced, where no minimum age of marriage exists, to bring the situation in line with the human rights standards discussed earlier. The focus of national law should be on safeguarding the rights of children and women and eliminating discrimination between males and females. Action to enact and enforce national and international laws on child marriage should include the following measures:

- Amend or introduce new legislation on child marriage and enforcement mechanisms where necessary, to guarantee 18 as the minimum age of marriage for both males and females and to address consent and appropriate sanctions.

- Review and amend, where necessary, national family and marriage laws and policies that discriminate against women and girls, so as to enhance their rights to property and economic independence.
- Enforce the registration of all births and marriages to support effective implementation of laws on minimum marriage age.
- Work towards the removal of reservations to key conventions, including CEDAW.
- Ensure that reports to international human rights treaty bodies, in particular the CRC and CEDAW, include a focus on measures adopted to delay child marriage and progress towards reducing child marriage.

Create an Enabling Environment for Social Change

Alongside the introduction of national laws, there needs to be a holistic policy environment that supports and promotes human rights, builds capacity and empowers individuals, community stakeholders and organizations to change attitudes and the cultural and religious norms that perpetuate child marriage. Changing entrenched social norms will require both national and community-level actions. In some contexts this will require different approaches at the community level. A flexible strategy – based on creating an enabling environment at the policy level, and ensuring adequate resources and incentives for meaningful social change at the community level – includes the following elements:

- Improve data and monitoring systems. Introduce mechanisms to enable regular monitoring of national laws and policies relating to child marriage to help assess progress. Listen and respond to the voices of child spouses and those at risk of child marriage when conducting situation analyses.

- Assess the role of customary and religious laws that condone child marriage and promote dialogue with traditional and religious leaders to identify practical ways to reduce child marriage.
- Train key government officials, judiciary, law enforcement officers and policy makers, at all levels, on the law and related gender equity and human rights to support the effective implementation and enforcement of the law and related policies.
- Support awareness-raising and public education programmes about the negative effects of child marriage, and related human rights of girls and women, to help change attitudes, and strengthen duties of parents, guardians and the community to protect vulnerable girls.
- Support civil society organizations, including financially, and ensure they have the skills and capacity to mobilize communities to end child marriage.
- Create opportunities for dialogue with men, including traditional and religious leaders, on women's and girls' rights within marriage, and discriminatory cultural norms.
- Establish global and national structures with a mandate to review laws and policies, monitor the practice, particularly within hotspots and advise on the formulation of relevant policies and programmes that will help promote the rights of married young women; and coordinate national efforts to end child marriages.

- Raise awareness within the international development community about the effects of child marriage on international development-agendas, including the MDGs, the Poverty Reduction Strategy Policies, and the landmark Cairo and Beijing women's human rights and development agendas.

Develop Multi-sectoral Programme Approaches and Partnerships

Given the multiple consequences of child marriage, a multi-sectoral and multi-pronged approach is the most effective way to address this issue. Girls at risk of child marriage and married young women will need different services and support. In addition, key support services such as reproductive health, education, law and employment need to work together at different levels, both national and community. Building alliances and working through partnerships and networks with multiple players is needed: from government agencies, civil society, researchers and human rights activists. The synergy of efforts will ensure effective policy and programme development and implementation.

- Strengthen the integration of child marriage prevention and support programmes into other government sector initiatives, especially in the areas of health, education, HIV and employment.
- Increase collaboration between civil society and national programmes to support, in particular, community-based efforts to reduce child marriage.
- Strengthen participation of key stakeholders in prevention programmes, in particular young people and community stakeholders, including parents, religious and community leaders and opinion makers, teachers and so on. Their participation is essential

in efforts to reinforce and implement policies and laws.

- Strengthen the role of community-based organizations, especially women's and young people's organizations, to enable them to engage better with community and religious leaders.
- Support health professionals to promote anti-child-marriage messages, and help them to mobilize at the community level, as these workers may be highly respected by communities. Health and reproductive health programmes and departments should play a key role in the development and implementation of policies on child marriage.
- Teachers in primary and secondary schools can help create an enabling environment for increased school enrolment of girls. Ensure that policies and programmes to improve school environments and the safety and retention of girls have full support from teachers.

Priority Areas for Policy and Programme Development

Initiatives at the national level aim to change policies and legislation, but at local and community levels, where traditions and customs reinforce child marriage, interventions should aim to change attitudes and behaviour, and improve entitlements. Efforts to deal with gender relations and reproductive health and rights should be based on sensitivity to local social dynamics, gaining the support of leaders and developing allies with local change agents. This includes the following components:

- Promote the right to education for all children, especially girls' rights to primary and secondary education.

- Introduce scholarships and other incentives to enable girls from poor and vulnerable communities to access education. Review and amend school policies that discriminate against married and pregnant girls. Address barriers within the school environment, including sanitary facilities and sexual violence, and ensure that the content of education is empowering and improves gender equality. In addition, train teachers to deal sensitively with at-risk girls and provide assertiveness advice for girls and support parents to send girls to school.
- Improve support for girls who escape child marriages through the creation of safety nets, such as the provision of shelters, education and health services that can address the specific needs and fears of married children.
- Provide support for economic and livelihood opportunities for girls and young women in rural communities. This can help ensure that marriage is not seen as the only option available to poor families. Credit schemes, growing in popularity across many developing countries, need to be more carefully thought out, so that they provide genuine alternatives to marriage and do not inadvertently encourage families to marry off girls in order to access credit schemes targeted only at married women.
- Ensure that child brides living with HIV are able to access new technologies for care, including antiretroviral drugs and communitybased care. This should include access to voluntary counselling and testing for couples.
- Ensure universal access to reproductive health services for all young people, in particular girls and young women. Provide access to family planning and

contraceptive services and information, and specialist services and care (including HIV and STI prevention, and obstetric care for fistula patients). Where possible introduce special initiatives to enable child brides and their spouses to negotiate effective use of contraception to help delay first births.

- Improve access to child and maternal health services, including antenatal and obstetric care, and child immunization and nutrition programmes, particularly for child wives/mothers who often have the least access to these services.
- Empower young women and girls, including married young women, and improve access to assertiveness skills and leadership programmes. Also create opportunities for their active engagement in all child marriage intervention programmes. Support individual girls to develop strategies to enable them to negotiate with families and resist child marriage.
- Combat all forms of violence against girls and women, especially sexual violence and abuse, through policies and programmes focusing on prevention, treatment, counselling and legal protection.
- Support grassroots advocacy that targets males within the community, in particular boys, young men, fathers and community gatekeepers such as religious and community leaders.
- Support and encourage families and communities who delay their children's marriage, and document and share community-based individual and collective interventions to end child marriage.

Strengthen Research and Data Collection Systems

The need for evidence-based policy making requires support for research that will provide both qualitative and quantitative information on child marriage. Data should be up to date, reliable, and reflect the voices and needs of child brides. Research institutions, particularly in resource-poor settings, should have the capacity to do this and research findings need to be disseminated at all levels to support policy and programme development. The following priority questions are provided to help guide research on child marriage:

- What are the determinants of child marriages in hotspot areas?
- What is the impact that laws have on the practice of child marriage?
- What is the impact of child marriage on the health of young women and infants?
- What indicators are needed to measure child marriage intervention programmes?
- What are the links between child marriage and key development concerns including education, maternal and child health, gender equality, poverty and HIV?

THE HISTORY OF CHILD ABUSE

The following speech was given at the National Parenting Conference in Boulder, Colorado, on September 25, 1997.

During the past three decades, I have spent much of my scholarly life examining primary sources such as diaries, autobiographies, doctor's reports, ethnographic reports and other documents that document what it must have felt like to have been a child--yesterday and today, in the East and the West, in literate and preliterate cultures.

In several hundred studies published by myself and my associates in The Journal of Psychohistory, we have provided extensive evidence that the history of childhood has been a nightmare from which we have only recently begun to awaken. The further back in history one goes--and the further away from the West one gets--the more massive the neglect and cruelty one finds and the more likely children are to have been killed, rejected, beaten, terrorized and sexually abused by their caretakers. Indeed, my conclusion from a lifetime of psychohistorical study of childhood and society is that the history of humanity is founded upon the abuse of children. Just as family therapists today find that child abuse often functions to hold families together as a way of solving their emotional problems, so, too, the routine assault of children has been society's most effective way of maintaining its collective emotional homeostasis.

Most historical families once practiced infanticide, erotic beating and incest. Most states sacrificed and mutilated their children to relieve the guilt of adults. Even today, we continue to arrange the daily killing, maiming, molestation and starvation of children through our social, military and economic activities. I would like to summarize here some of the evidence I have found as to why child abuse has been humanity's most powerful and most successful ritual, why it has been the cause of war and social violence, and why the eradication of child abuse and neglect is the most important social task we face today.

THE CHILD AS POISON CONTAINER

The main psychological mechanism that operates in all child abuse involves using children as what I have termed poison containers--receptacles into which adults project disowned parts of their psyches, so they can control these feelings in another body without danger to themselves. In good parenting, the child uses the caretaker as a poison container, much as it earlier used the mother's placenta as a poison container for cleansing its polluted blood. A good mother reacts with calming actions to the cries of a baby and helps it "detoxify" its dangerous emotions.

But when an immature mother's baby cries, she cannot stand the screaming, and strikes out at the child. As one battering mother put it, "I have never felt loved all my life. When the baby was born, I thought he would love me. When he cried, it meant he didn't love me. So I hit him. Rather than the child being able to use the parent to detoxify its fears and anger, the parent instead injects his or her bad feelings into the child and uses it to cleanse his or herself of depression and anger.

Consider a typical infanticidal, incestuous culture, the Bimin-Kuskusmin of New Guinea. As is so often true in pre-literate cultures, the mothers have long post-partum taboos against sex with their husbands, sleep naked against their children until they are about four years old, have orgasms while nursing them and regularly masturbate them. One three-year-old boy describes how whenever his mother was sad or angry she masturbated him so roughly that it hurt him, and he struggled to get away, complaining of a pain in his penis. "It hurts inside," he told the ethnologist. "It goes Œkoong, koong, koong' inside. I think it bleeds in there I don't like to touch it anymore. It hurts when I pee..." Sometimes, after his mother hurt him while masturbating him, he wounds himself in the thigh and abdomen with a sharp stick and draws blood, looking at his penis and saying, "Now it hurts here, outside, not in penis. Look, blood. Feels good...[2] Although he is only three years old, he understands quite well that he is being used as a poison container by his mother to relieve her depression. He says, "Mother twist penis, tight...Hurt inside...Mother angry, hurt Buuktiin's penis. Mother sad, hurt Buuktiin's penis...Mother not like Buuktiin's penis, want to cut off..."

Maternal incest and pederasty by men are quite common in pre-literate groups and were common in earlier historical times. Boys in many New Guinea groups today, for instance, are so traumatized by the early erotic experiences, neglect and assaults on their bodies that they need to prove their masculinity when they grow up and become fierce warriors and cannibals, with a third of them dying in raids and wars. In fact, I have found that rather than the incest taboo being universal--as anthropologists claim--it is incest itself that has been universal for most children in most cultures in most times. A childhood more or less free from adult sexual use is in fact a very late historical achievement, limited to a few fortunate children in a few modern nations. To give you some idea of the extensive evidence I have gathered for such an unlikely conclusion, I would like to begin by summarizing the evidence which exists for the sexual abuse of children around the world today.

THE SEXUAL ABUSE OF CHILDREN TODAY

In America, the most accurate scientific studies, based on lengthy interviews, report that 30 percent of men and 40 percent of women remember having been sexually molested during childhood---defining "molestation" as actual genital contact, not just exposure. About half of these are directly incestuous, with the family members, the other half usually being with others, but with the complicity of caretakers in at least 80 percent of the cases.

These experiences of seduction are not just pieced together from fragmentary memories, but are remembered in detail, are usually for an extended period of time and have been confirmed by follow-up reliability studies in 83 percent of the cases, so they are unlikely to have been fantasies. The seductions occurred at much earlier ages than had been previously assumed, with 81 percent occurring before puberty and an astonishing 42 percent under age 7.

As high as these molestation rates seem, however, they represent only a portion of the true rates, not only because those interviewed do not include populations that have been shown to have extremely high rates---such as criminals, prostitutes, juveniles in shelters, psychotics, etc.--but also because only conscious memories were counted, and the earliest seductions of children are almost never remembered except during psychotherapy. Adjusting statistically for what is known about these additional factors, I have concluded that the real sexual abuse rate for America is 60 percent for girls and 45 percent for boys, about half of these directly incestuous.

Other Western nations have made fewer careful studies. A recent Canadian study by Gallup of 2,000 adults has produced incidence rates almost exactly the same as those found in the United States. Latin American family sexual activity--particularly widespread pederasty as part of macho sexuality--is considered even more widespread. In England, a recent BBC "ChildWatch" program asked its female listeners--a large though admittedly biased sample--if they remembered sexual molestation, and, of the 2,530 replies analyzed, 83 percent remembered someone touching their genitals, 62 percent recalling actual intercourse.

In Germany, the Institut für Kindheit has recently concluded a survey asking West Berlin schoolchildren about their sexual experiences, and 80 percent reported having been molested.

Outside the West, the sexual molestation of children is a routine practice in most families. Childhood in India begins, according to observers, with the child being regularly masturbated by the mother, the girl "to make her sleep well," the boy "to make him manly." The child sleeps in the family bed, witnesses and most likely takes part in sexual intercourse between the parents. The child is often "borrowed" to sleep with other members of the extended household, leading to the Indian proverb that "For a girl to be a virgin at ten years old, she must have neither brothers nor cousin nor father." Childhood is so eroticized that, as one Western observer put it, "The little Hindu girls are deflowered by the little boys with whom they play, and repeat together the erotic lessons which their parents have unwittingly taught them on account of the general promiscuity of family life throughout India. In all the little girls of less than ten years of age the complete hymen is wanting...Incest is often the rule rather than the exception."

Child marriage was, of course, a long-standing Indian practice. When laws were passed in 1929 trying to outlaw it, the government was overwhelmed by men insisting that early marriage was an absolute necessity, since little girls were naturally very sexual and must be married early if they are to be restrained from seducing adults. "Cupid overtakes the hearts of girls...at an early age," they said. "A girl's desire for sexual intercourse is eight times greater than that of males."

Indian mothers also often supported early marriage, frankly admitting it was necessary in order to protect their little girls against rape in the family, saying that "they were afraid to leave their daughters at home, even for one afternoon, without a mother's eye and accessible to the men of the family."

The Indian subcontinent, in fact, still has many groups, such as the Baiga, where actual incestuous marriage is practiced, between fathers and daughters, between mothers and sons, between siblings and even between grandparents and their grandchildren--thus disproving the oft-repeated anthropological truism that "no known tribe has ever permitted incest" because if it were allowed society would surely cease functioning. In many of these villages, the children move at the age of 5 or 6 from the incestuous activities of the family bed to spend the rest of their childhood in sex dormitories, where they are initiated by older youth and men into intercourse with a succession of other children, none for longer than three days at a time, under threat of gang rape.

Childhood in China has historically had the same institutionalized rape rituals as in India, including the pederasty of boys, child concubinage, the castration of boys to be used sexually as eunuchs, marriage of young girls to a number of brothers, widespread boy and girl prostitution and the regular sexual use of child servants and slaves. So prevalent was the rape of little girls that Western doctors found that, as in India, few girls entering puberty had intact hymens. Even the universal practice of foot binding was for sexual purposes, with a girl undergoing extremely painful crushing of the bones of her feet for years in order that men could make love to her big toe as a fetish, a penis-substitute.

Childhood in contemporary Japan, although somewhat more Western than that of other Eastern nations, still includes masturbation by mothers "to put them to sleep." Parents often have intercourse with their children in bed with them, and "co-sleeping," with parents physically embracing the child, often continues until the child is ten or fifteen. One recent Japanese study found daughters sleeping with their fathers over 20 percent of the time after age 16. Recent sex surveys report memories of sexual abuse even higher than comparable American studies, and "hot lines" of sexual abuse report mother-son incest in almost a third of the calls, the mother saying to her teenage son, "It's not good to do it alone.

Your IQ becomes lower. I will help you, " or "You cannot study if you cannot have sex. You may use my body," or "I don't want you to get into trouble with a girl. Have sex with me instead." Historically, Japan has been one of the most endogamous societies in the world, with incestuous marriages in court circles being approved even in historical times and preferred sibling, cousin, uncle-niece and aunt-nephew marriages having been so extensive that genetics experts have discovered that the incestuous inbreeding has affected the size and health of the Japanese. Even today, there are rural areas in Japan where fathers marry their daughters when the mother has died or is incapacitated, "in accordance with feudal family traditions."

The sexual use of children in the Near East is as widespread as in the Far East. Historically, all the institutionalized forms of pedophilia which were customary in the Far East are documented extensively for the Near East, including child marriage, child concubinage, temple prostitution of both boys and girls, parent-child marriage (among the Zoroastrians), sibling marriage (quite common among Egyptians), sex slavery, ritualized pederasty and child prostitution. Masturbation in infancy is said to be necessary "to increase the size" of the penis, and older siblings are reported to play with the genitals of babies for hours at a time.

Mutual masturbation, fellatio and anal intercourse are also said to be common among children, particularly with the older boys using younger children as sex objects. The nude public baths (hammam) are particularly eroticized in many areas, being especially notorious as a place of homosexual acts, both male and female.

Girls are used incestuously even more often than boys, since females are valued so little. One report found 80 percent of Near Eastern women surveyed recalled having been forced into fellatio between the ages of 3 and 6 by older brothers, cousins, uncles and teachers. The girls rarely complain, since "if there is any punishment to be meted out, it will always end up by being inflicted on her." Arab women know that their spouses are pedophiles and prefer having sex with children to having sex with them. Their retribution comes as follows. When the girl is about 6 years old, the women of the house grab her, pull her thighs apart and cut off her clitoris and often also her labia with a razor, thus usually ending her ability to feel sexual pleasure forever. One Egyptian woman relates her memory of how it happened to her. After being used sexually by the men in her family during her early childhood, she says:

I was six years old that night when I lay in my bed, warm and peaceful...I felt something move under the blankets, something like a huge hand...another hand was clapped over my mouth to prevent me from screaming.

They carried me to the bathroom...I remember...a rasping metallic sound which reminded me of the butcher when he used to sharpen his knife...My blood was frozen in my veins...my thighs had been pulled wide apart...I felt that the rasping knife or blade was heading straight down towards my throat. Then suddenly the sharp metallic edge seemed to drop between my thighs and there cut off a piece of flesh from my body.

I screamed with pain despite the tight hand held over my mouth, for the pain was not just a pain, it was like a searing flame that went through my whole body. After a few moments, I saw a red pool of blood around my hips. I did not know what they had cut off from my body, and did not try to find out. I just wept, and called out to my mother for help. But the worst shock of all was when I looked around and found her standing by my side. Yes, it was her, I could not be mistaken, in flesh and blood, right in the midst of these strangers, talking to them and smiling at them.

A recent survey of Egyptian girls and women showed 97 percent of uneducated families and 66 percent of educated families still practiced clitoridectomy. Nor is the practice decreasing--UN reports estimate that more than 74 million females have been mutilated, with "more female children mutilated today than throughout history."

Clitoridectomy, like all sexual mutilations, is, I believe, an act of incest. If it is incest when a father rapes a daughter, it is also incest when parents assault their children by cutting off, sewing up, burning, flaying or gashing their genitals. In all these cases, the child is being used for the sadistic sexual pleasure of the parent. In fact, circumcision ceremonies are often followed by drinking parties that end in intercourse, so sexually arousing is the circumcision---in some areas, the traveling circumcizer is actually accompanied by some prostitutes, who know how sexually excited villages become after the ceremony. Therefore, the practice of sexually mutilating children's genitals---one of the most widespread rituals in the world--by itself makes incest a near-universal trait.

THE EVOLUTION OF CHILDHOOD

Historically, the routine use of children as poison containers to prevent adults from feeling overwhelmed by their anxieties has also been universal. Examples from the history of childhood regularly reveal children are expected to "absorb" the bad feelings of their caretakers. As one peasant community in rural Greece puts it, you must have children around to put your bad feelings into, especially when the "Bad Hour" comes around. An informant describes the process as follows:

One of the ways for the Bad Hour to occur is when you get angry. When you're angry a demon gets inside of you. Only if a pure individual passes by, like a child for instance, will the "bad" leave you, for it will fall on the unpolluted.

Newborn infants, in particular, were perfect poison containers because they were so "unpolluted." The newborn then became so full of the parent's projections that even if he or she is allowed to live (up to half the children in early societies were murdered at birth), the infant had to be tied up--tightly swaddled in bandages for up to a year or more--to prevent it from "tearing its ears off, scratching its eyes out, breaking its legs, or touching its genitals," i.e., to prevent it from acting out the violent and sexual projections of the parents.

Children were particularly useful as poison containers when adults felt anxious about recent or impending success. Success stirs up superego retaliation, and the sacrifice of children to appease the gods--that is, the punitive parents--was an extremely widespread guilt-reducing device. Most early states practiced child sacrifice. Typical was Carthage, where a large cemetery has been discovered called The Tophet filled with over 20,000 urns deposited there between 400 and 200 B.C. The urns contained bones of children sacrificed by their parents, who often would make a vow to kill their next child if the gods would grant them a favor--for instance, if their shipment of goods were to arrive safely in a foreign port. Some urns contain the bones of stillborn babies along with the bones of two-year-olds, indicating that if the promised child was not born alive, an older child had also to be killed to satisfy the promise.

The sacrifice was accompanied by a music, wild dancing and riotous orgy, and was probably accompanied by the ritual rape of virgin girls, as it was with the Incans. Plutarch told how the priests would "cut their throats as if they were so many lambs or young birds; meanwhile the mother stood by without a tear or moan [while] the whole area before the statue was filled with a loud noise of flutes and drums..." Sacrifice, rape and genital mutilation of young girls continues to take place today in the Andean mountains, particularly to ward off the guilt coming after successful cocaine deliveries. These ceremonies, from antiquity to today, resemble closely the satanic rituals made familiar recently in the newspapers, using the infliction of rape, sexual mutilation and other horrors in order to visit upon child victims elements of the traumas of the satanists' own childhood.

That child sacrifice was carried out mainly by the rich in each of these early societies confirms my theory that it is a guilt-reducing technique. Whenever new ventures were begun, children would be sacrificed. Whenever a new building or bridge was built, a child would be buried within it as a "foundation sacrifice." Children still play at capturing a child and making it part of the bridge in "London Bridge's Falling Down." Children's bodies were particularly useful in curing disease. Whatever one's physical ills, a child could be used to "absorb" the poison that was responsible. When, for instance, one wanted to be cured of leprosy, one was supposed to kill a child and wash one's body in its blood.

When one wanted to find out if a house whose previous occupants had died of plague was still infected or not, one rented some children to live in it for several weeks to see if they died--rather like the use of canaries in mines to detect poisonous gas. When one was impotent, depressed or had venereal disease, doctors prescribed having intercourse with a child. As late as the end of the nineteenth century, men who were brought into Old Bailey for having raped young girls were let go because "they believed that they were curing themselves of venereal disease."

Raping virgins was particularly effective for impotence and depression; as one medical book put it, "Breaking a maiden's seal is one of the best antidotes for one's ills. Cudgeling her unceasingly, until she swoons away, is a might remedy for man's depression. It cures all impotence." And, of course, whenever a parent had a disease, they always had their children handy to absorb the poison. Thus British doctors in the nineteenth century regularly found when visiting men who had venereal disease that their children also had the same disease--on their mouths, anuses or genitals.

No matter what anxieties one had, one had children always at hand to use to relieve them. The evolution of childhood from incest to love and from abuse to empathy has been a slow, uneven path, but one whose progressive direction is, I think, unmistakable. This evolution of parent-child relations is, I contend, an independent source of historical change, lying in the ability of successive generations of parents to live through their own childhood traumas a second time and work through their anxieties in a slightly better manner this second time around. It is in this sense that I say that history is like psychotherapy, which also heals through revisiting one's childhood traumas and reworking earlier anxieties. If the parent--the mother, for most of history--is given even the most minimal support by society, the evolution of childhood progresses, new variations in historical personality are formed, and history begins to move in new, innovative directions.

The crucial relationship in this evolution is the mother-daughter relationship. If little girls are treated particularly badly, they grow up to be mothers who cannot rework their traumas, and history is frozen. For instance, although China was ahead of the West in most ways during the pre-Christian era, it became "frozen" and fell far behind the West in evolutionary social and technological change after it adopted the practice of footbinding girls. Similarly, the cliterodectomy of girls in Moslem societies has inhibited their social development for centuries, since it likewise puts a brake on the ability of the next generation of mothers to make progress in caring for their children.

Clearly, different groups have moved different distances up the ladder of psychological evolution, since some contemporary groups still practice brain-eating as our Paleolithic ancestors did, and different subgroups of our more advanced nations still terrorize and abuse their children in ways identical to those that were commonplace centuries ago, producing the "historical fossils" (early "psychoclasses") we now call borderline personalities and other severe character disorders. Your neighbor is as likely to be a result of medieval parenting as of modern parenting, so modern societies contain a full range of childrearing modes and psychoclasses.

The "generational pressure" for psychological change is not only an independent historical force--originating in inborn adult-child striving for relationship--it occurs independent of social and technological change, and can be found even in periods of economic stagnation. My "psychogenic theory of history" posits that a society's childrearing practices are not just one item in a list of cultural traits, but--because all other traits must be passed down from generation to generation through the narrow funnel of childhood--instead makes childrearing the very basis for the transmission and development of all other cultural traits, placing definite limits on what can be achieved in the material spheres of history.

The main source of childhood evolution is, I believe, the process I call psychogenesis, by which parents--mainly the mother for most of history--revisit a second time around the stages of childhood and undo to some extent the traumas they themselves endured. It is in this sense that history is like a psychotherapy of the generations, undoing trauma and giving historical personality a chance at a new start with every baby born. Only humans have brain networks that allow this miracle to take place. All cultural changes in the past 100,000 years of Homo sapiens sapiens are epigenetic, not genetic.

Regardless of changes in the environment, it is only when changes in childhood occur that epigenetic changes in the brain can occur and societies can begin to progress and move in unpredictable new directions that are more adaptive. That more individuated and loving individuals are ultimately more adaptive is understandable--because they are less under the pressures of infantile traumas and are therefore more rational in reaching their goals. But that this childhood evolution--and therefore all social evolution--is terribly uneven is also understandable, given the varying conditions under which parents all over the world have to conduct their childrearing tasks.

THE SIX CHILDREARING MODES

The basic patterns of evolution of childhood have begun to be traced by myself and other psychohistorians. I would like to summarize the six childrearing modes that I have suggested are common to all groups that have traversed the full path of childhood and cultural evolution so far. These modes are, in fact, quite independent of technological development. But the overall evolutionary direction of parent-child relations is, I think, evident in the historical record, regardless of what labels one chooses to put on its stages. The earliest childrearing mode I have called infanticidal to highlight the constant presence of infanticidal wishes in the parent. Real infanticide is, of course, ubiquitous in most preliterate cultures, ranging about a third or more of all children born, and evidence remains of widespread infanticide among all historical records.

By historical times, census figures from antiquity show boy/girl ratios as high as 400 boys to 100 girls--a believable figure since, as Poseidippos said, "even a rich man always exposes a daughter." I have estimated that perhaps half of all children born in antiquity were killed by their caretakers, declining to about a third in medieval times and dropping to under one percent only by the eighteenth century. Since these skewed sex ratios do not vary by economic class--the rich do away with their children at about the same rates as the poor--the evidence suggests that the parents were coping with the emotional anxieties of childrearing more than economic conditions.

That incest is also traditional in the infanticidal mode is harder to prove conclusively, since what really happened in the family bed does not often leave historical traces. Yet all the records we have suggest that this was so. Man began, after all, as an incestuous primate--along with other primates, who remain incestuous today. In most simple societies today in such areas as New Guinea, boys and girls are used sexually by both their mothers and by the men, who gang rape girls and often are also pederasts who use the boys sexually, have boy-wives, or force all the boys to fellate them daily from age seven to fourteen "in order to ingest semen to counteract maternal pollution."

By the time historical records begin, the widespread sexual use of children is well documented. The Greek and Roman child lived his or her earliest years in an atmosphere of sexual abuse. Girls were commonly raped, as reflected in the many comedies that have scenes that were considered funny of little girls being raped. Both Greek and Roman doctors report that female children rarely have hymens--just like the Indian and Chinese girls I described above. In order to find out if your young wife was really a virgin (girls usually married before puberty to older men), one had to use mystical tests for virginity, since intact hymens were so rare.

Boys, too, were regularly handed over by their parents to neighboring men to be raped. Plutarch has a long essay on what was the best kind of person a father should give his son to for buggering. The common notion that this occurred only at "adolescence" is quite mistaken. It began around age seven, continued for several years and ended by puberty, when the boy's facial and pubic hairs began to appear. Child brothels, rent-a-boy services and sex slavery flourished in every city in antiquity. Children were so subject to sexual use by the men around them that schools were by law prohibited from staying open past sundown, so their pedagogues--slaves who were assigned to protect them against random sexual attack--could try to see that their teachers didn't assault them.

Petronius especially loved depicting adults feeling the "immature little tool" of boys, and Tiberius was said by Seutonius to have "taught children of the most tender years, whom he called his little fishes, to play between his legs while he was in his bath. Those which had not yet been weaned, but were strong and hearty, he set at fellatio..."

Since boys in antiquity shared the experience of being buggered, Christianity constructed its central myth of the Father sending his son down to be penetrated by a soldier's lance in order to restage the common experience of fathers giving their boys to a neighbor to be sexually penetrated. Those who accepted the myth, accepted the penetration, and were promised the Father's love and Mary's tears in return. Although Christianity attempted to reduce the outright killing of newborns, thus moving beyond the infanticidal mode, it continued the abandonment of children--whether by child sale or by sending to wet nurse or monastery or nunnery or foster family or to other homes as servants--which is why I labeled this second stage the abandoning mode.

The refusal of parents to raise their own legitimate children was so powerful that through the nineteenth century over half of the children born in Florence, for instance, were dumped into foundling homes at birth, to be picked up by their families--if they lived that long (the majority died)--when they were around five years old, thus avoiding having homes where crying babies disturbed the peace. The same abandonment was common in France, where, in 1900, over 90 percent of the babies born in Paris were carted out to the countryside to wetnurses at birth. As one author put it, "mother love" was a late historical achievement, not an instinctual trait.

Despite the advance that just abandoning rather than outright killing your children represents, most of the other childrearing practices of antiquity continued in the middle ages, with the buggering of boys--even in monasteries--continuing to be widespread and even accepted by society. By the time boys were in their teens, they were so addicted to violent sex that they sometimes formed adolescent raping gangs that grabbed and raped any girls or young women they could find unprotected, to such an extent that the majority of women in some cities would have been raped by these gangs at some time in their lives.

The erotic beating of children continued in Christian times, because of the anxieties of living with a child who is so full of your projections. Children were experienced as always about to turn into "changelings," those who, as St. Augustine puts it, "suffer from a demon"--which usually meant just that they cry too much, since the Malleus Maleficarum says that one can recognize changelings because they "always howl most piteously," and since Luther says they "are more obnoxious than ten children with their crapping, eating, and screaming."

That children with devils in them had to be beaten goes without saying. A panoply of beating instruments existed for that purpose, from cat-o'-nine tails and whips to shovels, canes, iron rods, bundles of sticks, the discipline (a whip made of small chains), the goad (shaped like a cobbler's knife, used to prick the child on the head or hands) and special school instruments like the flapper, which had a pear-shaped end and a round hole to raise blisters. The beatings described in the sources were almost always severe, involved bruising and bloodying of the body, began in infancy, were usually erotically tinged by being inflicted on bare parts of the body near the genitals and were a regular part of the child's daily life.

Century after century of battered children grew up to batter their own children in turn. Public protest was rare. Even humanists and teachers who had a reputation for gentleness approved of the severe beating of children. Those who attempted reform did so only to prevent death. As a thirteenth-century law said, "If one beats a child until it bleeds, then it will remember, but if one beats it to death, the law applies." As Batholomew Batty put it, parents must "keep the golden mean," which is to say they should not "strike and buffet their children about the face and head, and to lace upon them like malt sacks with cudgels, staves, fork or fire shovel," for then they might die of the blows. The correct way, he said, was to "Hit him upon the sides...with the rod, he shall not die thereof."

By the thirteenth century in the West, abandonment via oblation, or the giving of young children to monasteries for sexual and other uses, was ended, the first disapproval of pedophilia appeared, the first childrearing tracts were published and some advanced parents began to practice what I have termed the ambivalent mode of childrearing, where the child was not born completely evil, but was seen as being still full of enough dangerous projections so that the parent, whose task it was to mold it, must beat it into shape like clay.

Church moralists for the first time began to warn against sexual molestation of children by parents, nurses and neighbors (the mothers had previously been instructed to masturbate their boys "so their yards will grow long"). The length of time of swaddling was eventually reduced from a year or more to only a few months. Pediatrics and educational philosophy were born. Parents of means began suggesting that perhaps rather than sending their infants out to be wetnursed in some peasant village--and thereby condemning over half of them to early death--the mother might herself nurse her infant. The baby, said some mothers who began to try nursing their own babies, even responds to this care by giving love back to the nursing mother, stroking her breast and face and cooing. And if the father, as often happened, complained that his wife's breast belonged to him not the baby, these bold new mothers suggested that the father should be allowed to hold the baby too.

These childhood reforms immediately preceded and thereby produced the humanistic, religious and political revolutions we associate with early modern times. For the fifteenth and sixteenth centuries in Western Europe represent the great watershed of psychogenic change, wherein vastly improved childrearing allowed at least some of the schizoid and borderline personalities of antiquity and medieval times--who regularly heard voices and hallucinated visions--to move on to the more integrated, less splitting modern neurotic personality more familiar to recent times, thus achieving Melanie Klein's "depressive position."

The sixteenth-century watershed in childrearing allowed people to reduce splitting and feel real depression for the first time, as can be seen in the popularity of Renaissance melancholy (Hamlet's admirable depressive guilt), the ability of Protestants to end the good mother/bad mother splitting of Mary/Eve, and the ability to internalize the projective panoply of split Catholic saints/devils into Protestant depressive guilt. With this vast improvement in childrearing--in some families at least--the modern world could begin, with the development of science, technology and democratization now being possible in parts of the West.

By the seventeenth century, the intrusive mode of childrearing began, particularly in England, America and France, whereby the child was seen as less full of dangerous projections, so it could actually be unswaddled soon after birth, not given regular enemas (which had until then been given daily from birth to remove the bad contents felt to be inside the infant), toilet trained early rather than late, hit but not regularly whipped, and punished for masturbation rather than being masturbated by adults.

It eventually became unacceptable for men to go about with a mistress on one arm and a catamite on the other, though underground seduction of minors continued. Intrusive parenting, in essence, began to substitute psychological pressure for physical abuse, so that rather than whipping the child to prevent it from sin, it was, for instance, shut up in the dark closets for hours or left without food, sometimes for days. One mother shut her three-year-old boy up in a drawer. Another had a house she described as "a sort of little Bastille, in every closet of which was to be found a culprit--some were sobbing and repeating verbs, others eating their bread and water..." Another five-year-old French boy, in looking at a new apartment with his mother, told her, "Oh no, mama...it's impossible; there's no dark closet! Where could you put me when I'm naughty."

Although erotic whipping of children decreased gradually, the intrusive mode required nevertheless a steady pressure on the child to "break its will" and discipline it properly. This breaking of the will began early. John Wesley's mother said of her babies, "When turned a year old (and some before), they were taught to fear the rod, and to cry softly." One would never know, she claimed, that children were present in her house. Rousseau confirmed that in

France babies in their earliest days were often beaten to keep them quiet. Another mother wrote of her first battle with her four-month-old infant, "I whipped him til he was actually black and blue, and until I could not whip him any more, and he never gave up one single inch." One can sense in this description of baby battering the struggle with the mother's own powerful parent, with the baby seen as so obstinate that it "won the battle" even after being beaten. In fact, this "double image" of the child as both a powerful adult and a wicked child accounts for the merging of beater and beaten in our myriad historical accounts of child abuse. Here, for instance, is an early American father describing the beating of his four-year-old boy for not being able to read something. The child is first tied up naked in the cellar. Then, the father writes,

With him in this condition, and myself, the wife of my bosom, and the lady of my family, all of us in distress, and with hearts sinking within us, I commenced using the rod...During this most unpleasant, self denying and disagreeable work, I...felt all the force of divine authority and express command that I ever felt in any case in all my life...But under the all controlling influence of such a degree of angry passion and obstinacy, as my son had manifested, no wonder he thought he "should beat me out," feeble and tremulous as I was; and knowing as he did that it made me almost sick to whip him. At that he could neither pity me nor himself.

This picture of the merging of parent and child, with the father complaining that he is the one "beaten out" and in need of pity, is common for the intrusive mode. Similar confusion between parent and child can be seen in the severe punishments for masturbation championed by the child-training literature since Tissot. Prior to this, children were masturbated by adults and even licked on their bodies as though they were substitute breasts. For instance, Little

Louis XIII, in 1603, was described by his pediatrician as having his penis and breasts kissed by everyone in the court, and his parents would-regularly make him part of sexual intercourse in the royal bed.

But childrearing reformers beginning in the eighteenth century began to try to bring this open sexual abuse under control, only it was the child who was now punished for touching his or her genitals, under threat of circumcision, clitoridectomy, infibulation and various cages and other genital restraint devices.

These terrorizing warnings and surgical interventions only began to die out at the end of the nineteenth century, after two hundred years of brutal and totally unnecessary assault on children's bodies and psyches for touching themselves. Despite the reformers' efforts, progress was so uneven that one British journalist could write in 1924 that "cases of incest are terribly common in all classes. [Usually] the criminal...goes unpunished...Two men coming out from [an incest] trial were overheard saying to a woman who deplored there had been no conviction, ŒWhat nonsense! Men should not be punished for a thing like that. It doesn't harm the child.'"

It goes without saying that the effects on the child of these physical and psychological punishments were immense. Adults remembered that as children they had had recurring nightmares and even outright hallucinations as they lay awake at night, terrorized by imaginary ghosts, demons, "a witch on the pillow," "a large black dog under the bed," or "a crooked finger crawling across the room." History is filled with reports of children's convulsive fits, dancing manias, loss of hearing and speech, loss of memory, hallucinations of devils and confessions of intercourse with devils. Nor did the parents help their children's mental anguish by giving them comfort.

It was thought that the way for children to get over their fears was to make them face fear even more concretely, so adults used to take children on visits to the gibbet to inspect rotting corpses hanging there, while being told moral stories. Classes used to be taken out of school to witness hangings, and parents would also sometimes take their children to hangings and then beat them when they returned home to make them remember what they had seen. Even humanists, like Mafio Vegio, who protested the severe beating of children, would admit that "to let them witness a public execution is sometimes not at all a bad thing."

The effect on the children of this corpse-viewing was of course massive. One little girl, after her mother showed her the fresh corpse of her nine-year-old friend as an example, went around saying, "They will put daughter in the deep hole, and what will mother do?" Another woke at night screaming after seeing hangings, and "practiced hanging his own cat." Religion was a further source of terrorizing. God was said to "hold you over the pit of hell, much as one holds a spider, or some loathsome insect, over the fire" and children's books depicted Hell as follows: "The little child is in this red-hot oven. Hear how it screams to come out...It stamps its little feet on the floor..." Various terrorizing figures were used to control the child. If you were bad, the werewolf would gulp you down, Blue Beard would chop you up, Boney (Bonaparte) would eat your flesh, the black man or the chimney sweep would steal you away at night. This need to personify punitive figures was in fact so powerful that adults actually dressed up dummies to use in frightening children. As one English writer, in 1748, explained the practice:

The nurse takes a fancy to quiet the peevish child, and with this intent, dresses up an uncouth figure, makes it come in, and roar and scream at the child in ugly disagreeable notes, which grate upon the tender organs of the ear, and at the same time, by its gesture and near approach, makes as if it would swallow the infant up.

Another writer, in 1882, described how the nurse of a friend's child wanted to leave for the evening while the parents were out, and so told the little girl that a horrible Black Man...was hidden in the room to catch her the moment she left her bed...[Then] she made a huge figure of a black man with frightful staring eyes and an enormous mouth, and placed it at the foot of the bed where the little innocent child was fast asleep. As soon as the evening was over...[she] went back to her charge. Opening the door quietly, she beheld the little girl sitting up in her bed, staring in an agony of terror at the fearful monster before her, both hands convulsively grasping her fair hair. She was stone dead!

By the nineteenth century's socializing mode, some parents no longer needed to terrorize, beat and sexually seduce their children, and more gentle psychological means began to be used to "socialize" the child. The socializing mode is still the main model of upbringing in Western nations, featuring the mother as trainer and the father as provider and protector, and the child is seen as slowly being made to conform to the parents' model of goodness.

Many of the abusive practices are reduced in the home but remain elsewhere in society. While Elizabeth I was sexually seduced as a girl by her caretakers and Louis XV had Madame du Barry procure little girls for the King to rape in his royal bedroom, by the nineteenth century parents would less often commit incest themselves but still sent their children to schools where they were erotically whipped on the bare buttocks and usually buggered by the older boys and masters. As John Addington Symonds reported his experience as a boy at public school:

Every boy of good looks had a female name, and was recognized either as a public prostitute or as some bigger fellow's Œbitch.' Bitch was the word in common usage to indicate a boy who yielded his person to a lover. The talk in the dormitories and the studies was incredibly obscene. Here and there one could not avoid seeing acts of onanism, mutual masturbation, or the sports of naked boys in bed together.

Reformers during the nineteenth century tried to bring the rest of society into the socializing mode by legislation designed to prevent outright battering and sexual abuse of children, which of course still went on in the majority of families around them. But those who tried to oppose buggering and beating boys in schools were opposed by parents who said "It didn't hurt me." Those who tried to pass child labor legislation to reduce horrendous working conditions and hours were labeled Communists. And those who thought one could bring up children kindly were considered impractical visionaries.

Even so, the decrease in parental seduction and beating during the intrusive mode produced an explosion of social innovation, allowing nations to produce the democratic and industrial revolutions of the modern period. As Hanns Sachs pointed out long ago in his paper "The Delay of the Machine Age," when people in antiquity first invented the steam engine, they dared to use it only for children's toys. It was only after fifteen centuries of childrearing evolution that steam could finally begin to be used by less fearful and more individuated adults to provide power for the benefit of mankind. As hellfire and physical discipline were replaced by other childrearing methods, it was the socializing psychoclass that built the modern world, with its democratic, innovative and class-dominated society.

What kind of society might be envisioned by children brought up under the latest childrearing mode--what I have termed the helping mode--whereby a minority of parents are now trying to help their children reach their own goals at each stage of life, rather than socializing them into adult goals--is yet to be seen. I suspect it will be far less class-centered and more empathic of others than is the socializing modern world with which we are familiar.

That helping mode children grow up to be incapable of creating wars is also becoming evident from watching the anti-war activities of my children and those of their friends who have been brought up by other helping mode parents. For war is only understandable as a sacrificial ritual in which young men are sent by their parents to be hurt and killed as representatives of the independence-seeking parts of themselves. Psychohistorians have regularly found that images on the magazine covers and in political cartoons in the months prior to wars reveal fears of the nation becoming "too soft" and vulnerable, with images of dangerous women threatening to engulf and hurt people.

These regressed group-fantasies eventually produce so much anxiety that a sacrifice of innocent victims is deemed necessary, and another nation who also needs a sacrifice is located. So regular are these group-fantasies in the media that I was able to forecast, for instance, the recent Persian Gulf War months before Iraq invaded Kuwait by locating in the American media an upsurge in imagery of devouring mommies and guilty children needing punishment.

THE TASK OF THE FUTURE

That all social violence--whether by war, revolution or economic exploitation--is ultimately a consequence of child abuse should not surprise us. The propensity to reinflict childhood traumas upon others in socially-approved violence is actually far more able to explain and predict the actual outbreak of wars than the usual economic motivations, and we are likely to continue to undergo our periodic sacrificial rituals of war if the infliction of childhood trauma continues. Clear evidence has been published in The Journal of Psychohistory that the more traumatic one's childhood, the more one is likely to be in favor of military solutions to social problems.

Technologically, the human race is now quite able to satisfy its needs--if we can live together without violence. But unless we now employ our social resources toward consciously assisting the evolution of childrearing, we will be doomed to the periodic destruction of our resources, both material and human. To Selma Freiberg's dicta that "Trauma demands repetition" I would only add "repetition in social behavior." We cannot be content to only continue to do endless repair work on damaged adults, with more jails and police and therapists and political movements. Our task now must be to create an entirely new profession of "child helpers" who can reach out to every new child born on earth and help its parents give it love and independence.

Such a parent outreach movement is already under way in a few cities, and special issues of The Journal of Psychohistory have been published to document its operation. A special issue on "Changing Childhood" is the most recent to be published, showing the success of parent outreach projects in several states. The success of parenting centers such as the one pioneered in Boulder, Colorado, for instance, has been astonishing. Through parenting classes and home visiting by paraprofessionals, they have measurably reduced child abuse, as shown by careful followup studies and by reduced police reports and hospital entrance rates.

All this has been accomplished with very small monetary outlays, since these parent outreach centers operate mainly with volunteer labor, while it has the potential to save trillions of dollars annually in the costs of social violence, police enforcement, jails and other consequences of the widespread child abuse of today.

Such a parent support movement would resemble the universal education movement of over a century ago. People then objected to providing universal education, by saying, "Well, yes, perhaps free education is useful for all children--but that would require hiring millions of teachers. How can we afford it?" We, too, admit that we will eventually need millions of parent helpers to teach parents how to bring up children and produce non-violent adults. But the teaching of parenting is just the unfinished half--the most important half--of the free education movement of the past, with its goal the empowerment of children to realize their innate capacities for love and work.

Changing childhood is a communal task. And it works. In 1979, Sweden passed a law saying that hitting children was as unlawful as hitting adults! Imagine the audacity! Children were people, just like adults! Parents who hit their children weren't put into jail--that would just deprive the children of their caretakers. But the parents were taught how to bring up children without hitting them. And at the same time, high school students were taught how to bring up children without violence. By now, 20 years later, these high school students have their own children, and...surprise! They don't hit them! To those who object to the cost of communities helping all parents, we can only reply: Can we afford not to teach parenting?

What more important task can we devote our resources to? Do we really want to have massive armies and jails and emotionally crippled adults forever? Must each generation continue to torture and neglect its children so they repeat the violence and economic exploitation of previous generations? Why not achieve meaningful political and social revolution by first achieving a parenting revolution? If war, social violence, class domination and economic destruction of wealth are really revenge rituals for childhood trauma, how else can we remove the source of these rituals? How else end child abuse and neglect? How else increase the real wealth of nations, our next generation? How else achieve a world of love and laughter of which we are truly capable?

THE POLITICAL CONSEQUENCES OF CHILD ABUSE

Although centuries of novels and autobiographies have dealt with the subject of child abuse in all its forms, society has been slow in recognizing the frequency with which this assault is committed. Only in the last twenty years has there been any real progress in this respect, and most of it is due to the efforts of a small number of researchers and above all to the media. Still underestimated and sometimes contested are the consequences very early abuse will have for the victims in their adult lives.

The issues involved have been largely ignored, and there is correspondingly little mention of them in historical and anthropological studies. Thus sociologist Wolfgang Sovsky is able to write an otherwise impressive work on forms of violence without making one single reference to the childhood dimension. He gives very considerable space to the willful infliction of suffering, calling it "mysterious," although it is readily explicable once we countenance the idea that the bodies of the executioners, torturers and the orchestrators of organized manhunts may have learned their fateful lessons very early and thus very effectively.

Also Goldhagen restricts himself to a phenomenological discussion of the people who volunteered to torture and humiliate others, without giving any consideration to their childhood. He does devote much attention to the emotions of the perpetrators, a subject hitherto largely ignored, but without the background of their early upbringing their behavior still remains mysterious. The reader seeks in vain for an explanation. What made respected members of society suddenly act like monsters? How could a former teacher like Klaus Barbie, and other men described by their daughters as kind, caring fathers, have innocent people tortured or indeed do the torturing themselves? Goldhagen does not address this question. He is obviously convinced that references to traditional anti--Semitism in Germany provide a satisfactory answer. They do not.

The hypothesis that German anti--Semitism was the real reason for the Holocaust has been rightly criticized by urging a comparison with the First World War. At that time anti--Semitism was just as strong in Germany but no organized genocide resulted. And why no Holocaust in the other anti--Semitic countries‹Poland, Russia and other parts of Europe? The argument that in the Weimar Republic unemployment and poverty caused immense general frustration that was discharged via the mass murder of the Jews is hardly convincing, given that Hitler was quickly successful in getting unemployment under control.

There must have been other factors at play which have hitherto been ignored, factors going some way to explaining why the Holocaust happened in Germany and why it happened at this particular time rather than another. In my view, one possible operative factor is the destructive child--rearing style practiced widely on infants around the turn of the century in Germany, a style I have no hesitation in referring to as a universal abuse of infants.

Of course children in other countries have been and still are mistreated in the name of upbringing or caregiving, but hardly already as babies and hardly with the systematic thoroughness characteristic of the Prussian pedagogy. In the two generations before Hitler's rise to power, the implementation of this method was brought to a high degree of perfection in Germany. With this foundation to build on, Hitler finally achieved what he wanted: "My ideal of education is hard. Whatever is weak must be hammered away. In the fortresses of my militant order a generation of young people will grow to strike fear into the heart of the world. Violent, masterful, unafraid, cruel youth is what I want. Young people must be all that.

They must withstand pain. There must be nothing weak or tender about them. The free--magnificent predator must flash from their eyes again. I want them strong and beautiful...That way I can fashion things anew." This education program revolving on the extermination of everything life--giving was the forerunner of Hitler's plans for the extermination of an entire nation. Indeed it was the prerequisite for the ultimate success of his designs.

The numerous and widely--read tracts by Dr. Daniel Gottlieb Moritz Schreber, the inventor of the Schrebergärten (the German world for small allotments) are of major interest here. Some of them ran to as many as 40 editions, and their central concern was to instruct parents in the systematic upbringing of infants from the very first day of life.

Many people motivated by what they thought to be the best of intentions complied with the advice given them by Schreber and other authors about how best to raise their children if they wanted to make them into model subjects of the German Reich.

They did this without even remotely suspecting that they were exposing their children to a systematic form of torture with long--term effects. Germany sayings and catch--phrases like "Praise be to the things that make us tough" and "What doesn't kill us will strengthen us," still to be heard from educationists of the old school, probably originated in this period.

Morton Schatzman, who quotes highly enlightening passages from Schreber's writings, is of the opinion that here we are in the presence not of child--raising methods but of systematic instruction in child persecution. One of Schreber's convictions is that when babies cry they should be made to desist by the use of "physically perceptible admonitions," assuring his readers that "such a procedure is only necessary one, or at the most twice, and then one is master of the child for all time. From then on, one look, one single threatening gesture will suffice to subjugate the child." Above all, the newborn child should be drilled from the very first day to obey and to refrain from crying.

Today, people who have been brought up in anything even remotely approaching a humane way will hardly be able to imagine the rigor and tenacity with which Schreber himself implemented this program. Psychoanalyst Wilhelm G. Niederland quotes examples that cast light on the everyday practical conduct of child--rearing in those decades‹for example, recipes for inculcating the "art of self--denial" into infants.

"The method should be simple and effective: the child is placed on the lap of its nanny while the latter is eating or drinking whatever takes her fancy. However urgent the infant's oral needs may become in this situation, they must not be gratified."

Niederland quotes an account by Schreber from his own family life. A nanny eating pears while holding one of his children on her lap was unable to resist the temptation of giving the infant a slice. She was immediately dismissed. The news of this draconian measure quickly spread to all the other nannies in Leipzig, and from that time on, writes Schreber, he "never again encountered such insubordination, neither with that child nor with any of the others that came later."

Contrary to received opinion prevalent as recently as 15 years ago, the human brain at birth is not fully developed. The abilities a person's brain develops depend on experiences in the first three years of life. Studies on abandoned and severely mistreated Romanian children revealed striking lesions in certain areas of the brain and marked emotional and cognitive insufficiencies in later life. According to very recent neurobiological findings, repeated traumatization leads to an increased release of stress hormones that attack the sensitive tissue of the brain and destroy existing neurons. Other studies of mistreated children have revealed that the areas of the brain responsible for the "management" of emotions are 20 to 30 percent smaller than in normal persons.

The children systematically subjected to obedience drill around the turn of the century were not only exposed to corporal "correction" but also to severe emotional deprivation. The upbringing manuals of the day described physical demonstrations of affection such as stroking, cuddling and kissing as indications of a doting, mollycoddling attitude. Parents were warned of the disastrous effects of spoiling their children, a form of indulgence entirely incompatible with the prevalent ideal of rigor and severity. As a result, infants suffered from the absence of direct loving contact with the parents. The best they could hope for was to find some kind of substitute from the servants, who in numerous cases used and exploited them as objects of pleasure, thus frequently adding to the children's emotional confusion.

Since the experiments conducted on monkeys by Dr. Harlow in the Fifties, we know that animals raised by artificial "robot" mothers later turned aggressive and showed no interest in their own offspring. New research on macaque monkeys revealed that they kill even members of their own species if they were brought up without appropriate care. John Bowlby's studies on the absence of early attachment in delinquents and René Spitz' descriptions of small children dying of hospitalism following emotional neglect during hospitalization under extremely hygienic conditions are indications that not only animal but also human babies require reassuring sensory contact with their parents if socialization is to take a normal course.

These findings presented bv Bowlby and Spitz almost 40 years ago are corroborated by recent neurobiological research. The studies in question suggest that not only active battering but also the absence of loving physical contact between child and parent will cause certain areas of the brain, notably those responsible for the emotions, to remain underdeveloped. Hence the children "subjugated by looks" suffered emotional harm that was only to develop its full destructive potential in the next generation.

Present--day neurobiological research makes it easier for us to understand the way Nazis like Eichmann, Himmler, Höss and others functioned. The rigorous obedience training they underwent in earliest infancy stunted the development of such human capacities as compassion and pity for the sufferings of others. They were incapable of emotion in the face of misfortune, such feelings were alien to them. Their total emotional atrophy enabled the perpetrators of the most heinous crimes imaginable to function "normally" and to continue to impress their environment with their efficiency in the years after the war without the slightest remorse. Dr. Mengele could perform the most cruel experiments on Jewish children in Auschwitz and then live for 30 years like a "normal," well--adjusted man.

In the absence of positive factors, affection and helping witnesses, the only course open to the mistreated individual is the disavowal of personal suffering and the idealization of cruelty with all its devastating after--effects. Undergoing an exceedingly humiliating and cruel upbringing at the preverbal stage, usually without helping witnesses, may instill into the victim admiration of this cruelty if there is no one in the immediate vicinity of the child to query those methods and stand-up for humane values. People subjected to mistreatment in childhood may go on insisting all their lives that beatings are harmless and corporal punishment is salutary although there is overwhelming, indeed conclusive evidence to the contrary. Vice versa, a child protected, loved and cherished from the outset will thrive on that experience for a lifetime.

Binjamin Wilkomirski, the author of a harrowing and intensely illuminating book about his childhood in the concentration camps, once confided to me in a personal encounter some observations made with the eyes of an imprisoned but extremely wide--awake child on the behavior of the female camp guards. He said that it had taken him 50 years to inquire who those "blokowas" really were, those women who had so openly and unreservedly relished the job of tormenting and humiliating Jewish children and subjecting them to every conceivable variety of mental and physical cruelty.

To his astonishment, perusal of the trial records revealed that most of them were young women between 19 and 21 who had formerly had quite ordinary jobs as seamstresses or sales clerks and whose biographies contained nothing in any way unusual. During the trial they unanimously claimed that they had not been aware that Jewish children were human beings. The conclusion that immediately suggests itself is that ultimately propaganda and manipulation are sufficient to transform people into sadistic executioners and mass murderers.

This is not an opinion I share. On the contrary. It is my belief that only men and women who had experienced mental and physical cruelty in the first weeks and months of life and had been shown no love at all could possibly have let themselves be made into Hitler's willing executioners. As Goldhagen's archive material shows, they needed next to no ideological indoctrination because their bodies knew exactly what they wanted to do as soon as they were allowed to follow their inclinations. And as the Jews, young or old, had been declared non--persons, there was nothing to stop them indulging those inclinations.

But no amount of indoctrination alone, at school or wherever, will unleash hatred in a person who has no preconditions in that direction. It is well known that there were also Germans, like Karl Jaspers, Hermann Hesse or Thomas Mann, who immediately recognized the declaration that Jews were non--persons as an alarm signal and the rallying cry of untrammeled barbarism.

For people like the "blokowas," exposed to emotional confusion in their early childhood, the declaration was a highly convenient expedient. All they needed to do was refuse the children water to wash themselves and that gave them sufficient reason to hate them for being dirty and coal--black. They could toss lumps of sugar to starving children and then despise them for the alacrity with which they scrambled to pick them up. Those young women could turn the children into precisely what they needed to feel powerful and could thus vent on their victims the old, unconscious rage slumbering within them.

However brutally these people were brought up, they showed no immediate signs of the harm done to them. On the contrary. Many of them grew up into seemingly well--adjusted young people. But sooner or later, usually one generation later, when the tormented children had themselves become parents, the former victims did the same with their children as had been done to them, with no feelings of guilt. It was the only thing they knew, after they had repressed and denied their own pain.

Studying child abuse confronts us with the astonishing fact that parents will inflict the same punishment or neglect on their children as they experienced themselves in their early lives. But as adults they have no recollection of what they went through. In the case of sexual assault on children, it is quite usual for the perpetrators to have no conscious knowledge of their own early life--history or at the least to be cut off from the attendant feelings aroused by those experiences. It is not until they are in therapy‹always supposing they are given any‹that it transpires that they have been reenacting what they went through as children.

The sole explanation I can advance for this fact is that information on the cruelty suffered in childhood remains stored in the brain in the form of unconscious memories. For a child, conscious experience of such treatment is impossible. If children are not to break down completely under the pain and the fear, they must repress that knowledge. But the unconscious memories drive them to reproduce those repressed scenes over and over again in the attempt (and with the false hope) to liberate themselves of the fears that cruelty and abuse have left with them. The victims create situations in which they can assume the active role in order to master the feeling of helplessness and escape the unconscious anxieties.

But this liberation is a specious one because the effects of the past don't change as long as they remain unnoticed. Over and over again the perpetrator will go in search of new victims. As long as one projects hatred and fear onto scapegoats, there is no way of coming to terms with those feelings. Not until the cause has been recognized and the natural reaction to wrongdoing understood can the blind hatred wreaked on innocent victims be dissipated. The function it performs, that of masking the truth, is no longer necessary. Sex criminals who have worked through their lives in therapy may no longer run the risk of a destructive reenactment of their traumas. What is hatred? As I see it, it is a possible consequence of the rage and despair that cannot be consciously felt by a child which has been neglected and mistreated even before he or she has learned to speak. As long as the anger directed at a parent or other first caregiver remains unconscious or disavowed, it cannot be dissipated. It can only be taken out on oneself or stand--ins, on scapegoats such as one's own children or alleged enemies. Sympathetic observation of the cries of an infant brings home forcibly to the onlooker how intense the feelings involved must be. The hatred can finally work as a life--saving defense against the life--threatening powerlessness.

The studies at my disposal already in 1980 and referred to in my book For Your Own Good confirmed my conjecture that, both in Nazi Germany and among the professional American soldiers who voluntarily served in Vietnam, brutally--raised children figured prominently among the most vindictive war criminals. Further confirmation was brought by study of the childhood biographies of those exceptional people who in times of terror had the courage to rescue others from extermination.

Why were there people brave enough to risk their lives to save Jews from Nazi Persecution? Much scientific inquiry has been expended on this question. The usual answers revolve around religious or moral values such as Christian charity or a sense of responsibility instilled in them by parents, teachers and other caregivers. But there is no doubt that the active supporters of the extermination and the passive hangers--on had usually also been given a religious upbringing. So this can hardly furnish a sufficient explanation.

I was convinced that there must have been some special factor in the childhood of the rescuers, in the prevailing atmosphere of their childhood, that made it so fundamentally different from what the war criminals had experienced, but at first I couldn't prove my hypothesis. For years I sought in vain for a book that would give this subject adequate coverage. Finally, thanks to Lloyd deMause's help, I found an empirical study by the Oliners, The Altruistic Personality: Rescuers of Jews in Nazi Europe, based on interviews with more than 400 witnesses ot those dark days. It confirmed my hypothesis. The study concluded that the only factor distinguishing the rescuers from the persecutors and hangers--on was the way they had been brought up by their parents.

Almost all rescuers interviewed reported that their parents had attempted to discipline them with arguments rather than punishment. They were only rarely subjected to corporal punishment, and if they were it was invariably in connection with some misdemeanor and never because their parents had felt the need to discharge some uncontrollable and inexplicable feeling of rage on them. One man recalled that he had once been spanked for taking smaller children out onto a frozen lake and endangering their lives. Another reported that his father had only ever hit him once and apologized afterwards. Many of the statements might be paraphrased thus: "My mother always tried to explain what was wrong about whatever it was I had done. My father also spent a lot of time talking to me. I was impressed by what he had to say."

What a different picture we get from the reports of the persecutors and hangers--on: "When my father was drunk he took the whip to me. I never knew what I was being beaten for. Often it was for something I had done months before. And when mother was in a temper she tore into anyone who got in her way, including me."

Unlike such uncontrolled affective discharges subjectively felt to be justified, explaining what the parent feels is wrong is synonymous with trust in the otherwise good intentions of the child. Such a course is motivated by respect and faith in the child's ability to develop and change its behavior for the better.

People given early affection and support are quick to emulate the sympathetic and autonomous natures of their parents. Common to all the rescuers were self--confidence, the ability to take immediate decisions and the capacity for empathy and compassion with others. Seventy percent of them said that it only took them a matter of minutes to decide they wanted to intervene. Eighty percent said they did not consult anyone else. "I had to do it, I could never have stood idle and watched injustice being done."

This attitude, prized in all cultures as "noble," is not something instilled in children with fine words. If the behavior actually displayed by caretakers is such as to contradict their own words, if children are spanked in the name of lofty ideals, as is still the custom in some parochial schools, then those elevated sentiments are doomed to go unheard or even to provoke rage and violence. The children may end up aping those high--minded phrases and mouthing them in later life, but they will never put them into practice because they have no example to emulate.

Martin Luther, for example, was an intelligent and educated man, but he hated all Jews and he encouraged parents to beat their children. He was no perverted sadist like Hitler's executioners. But 400 years before Hitler he was disseminating this kind of destructive counsel. According to Eric Ericson's biography, his mother beat him severely before he was treated this way by his father and his teacher. He believed this punishment had "done him good" and was therefore justified. The conviction stored in his body that if parents do it then it must be right to torment someone weaker than yourself left a much more lasting impression on him than the divine commandments and the Christian exhortations to love your neighbor and be compassionate toward the weak.

Similar cases are discussed by Philip Greven in his highly informative book, Spare the Child. He quotes various American men and women of the church recommending cruel beatings for infants in the first few months of life as a way of ensuring that the lesson thus learnt remains indelibly impressed on them for the rest of their lives. Unfortunately they were only too right. These terrible destructive texts which have misled so many parents are the conclusive proof of the long--lasting effect of beating. They could only have been written by people who were exposed to merciless beatings as children and later glorified what they had been through. Fortunately, these books were not published in 40 editions in the USA.

An animal will respond to attack with "fight or flight." Neither course is open to an infant exposed to aggression from immediate family members. Thus the natural reaction remains spent up, sometimes for decades, until it can be taken out on a weaker object. Then the repressed emotions are unleashed against minorities. The targets vary from country to country. But the reasons for that hatred are probably identical the world over.

We know that as a boy Hitler was tormented, humiliated and mocked by his father, without the slightest protection from his mother. We also know that he denied his true feelings toward his father. The real sources of his hatred thus become obvious. I had gone in search of the true motives not only for Hitler's mental make--up but also that of many other dictators. In all of them I identified the effects of hatred of a parent that remained unconscious not only because hating one's father was strictly prohibited but also because it was in the interests of the child's self--preservation to maintain the illusion of having a good father. Only in the form of a deflection onto others was hatred permitted, and then it could flow freely. Hitler would hardly have found so much support if the "caregiving" patterns he had been exposed to and their detrimental after--effects had not been so widespread in Germany and Austria.

But Hitler's specific problems with the Jews can in fact be traced back to the period before his birth. In her youth, his paternal grandmother had been employed in a Jewish merchant's household in Graz. After her return home to the Austrian village of Braunau, she gave birth to a son, Alois, later to become Hitler's father, and received child--support payments from the family in Graz for 14 years. This story, which is recounted in many biographies of Hitler, represented a dilemma for the Hitler family. They had an interest in denying that the young woman had been left with child either by the Jewish merchant or his son. On the other hand, it was impossible to assert that a Jew would pay alimony for so long without good reason. Such generosity on the part of a Jew would have been inconceivable for the inhabitants of an Austrian village. Thus the Hitler family was faced with the insoluble dilemma of devising a version that would serve to nullify their "disgrace."

For Alois Hitler the suspicion that he might be of Jewish descent was insufferable in the context of the anti--Jewish environment he grew up in. All the plaudits he earned himself as a customs officer were insufficient to liberate him from the latent rage at the disgrace and humiliation visited on him through no fault of his own. The only thing he could do with impunity was to take out this rage on his son Adolf. According to the reports of his daughter of his former marriage, Angela, he beat his son mercilessly every day. In an attempt to exorcise his childhood fears, his son nurtured the maniac delusion that it was up to him to free not only himself of Jewish blood but also all Germany and later the whole world. Right up to his death in the bunker, Hitler remained a victim of this delusion because all his life his fear of his half--Jewish father had remained locked in his unconscious mind.

I have set out these ideas in greater detail in my book, For Your Own Good. Many people have told me that they found them highly unsettling and in no way sufficient to explain Hitler's actions.

Not all his actions, perhaps, but certainly his delusions. And those delusions are at the very least the foundation of his actions. I can certainly picture the boy Hitler swearing vengeance on "the Jews," those monstrous fantasy--figures of an already diseased imagination. Consciously, he probably thought he could have led a happy life if "the Jew" had not plunged his grandmother into the disgrace that he and his family had to live with. And it was this that in his eyes served to excuse the batterings he received from his father, who after all was himself a victim of the evil and omnipotent Jew. In the mind of an angry, seriously confused child, it is only a short step from there to the idea that all Jews should be exterminated.

Not only Jews. In the household of Hitler's family lived for years the very unpredictable schizophrenic aunt Johanna whose behavior is reported to be very frightening to the child. As an adult, Hitler ordered to kill every handicapped and psychotic person to free Germany society from this burden. Germany seemed for him to symbolize the innocent child who had to be saved. Consequently, Hitler wanted to protect his nation from the dangers he himself had had to face. Absurd? Not at all. For an unconscious mind, this kind of symbolization might sound very normal and logical.

Besides the sources of his fears connected with father and aunt, there was his early relationship with his very intimidated mother who lived in constant fear of her husband's violent outbursts and beatings. She called him "Uncle Alois" and endured patiently his humiliating treatment without any protest. Adolf's mother had lost the first three children due to an illness, and Adolf was her first child to survive infancy. We can easily imagine that the milk he drank from his mother was in a way "poisoned" by her own fear. He drank her milk together with her fears, but was of course unable to understand nor to integrate them.

These irrational fears‹that an outside, watching his speeches on videos can easily recognize‹stayed unrecognized and unconscious to Hitler until the end of his life. Stored up in his body, they drove him constantly to new destructive actions, in his endless attempt to find an outcome.

In the lives of all the tyrants I examined, I found without exception paranoid trains of thought bound up with their biographies in early childhood and the repression of the experiences they had been through. Mao had been regularly whipped by his father and later sent 30 million people to their deaths, but he hardly ever admitted the full extent of the rage he must have felt toward his own father, a very severe teacher who had tried through beatings to "make a man" out of his son. Stalin caused millions to suffer and die because even at the height of his power his actions were determined by unconscious infantile fear of powerlessness.

Apparently his father, a poor cobbler from Georgia, attempted to drown his frustration with liquor and whipped his son almost every day. His mother displayed psychotic traits, was completely incapable of defending her son and was usually away from home either praying in church or running the priest's household. Stalin idealized his parents right up to the end of his life and was constantly haunted by the fear of dangers that had long since ceased to exist but were still present in his deranged mind. The same might be true of many other tyrants.

The groups of people they singled out for persecution and the rationalization mechanisms they employed were different in each case, but the fundamental reason behind it was probably identical. They often drew on ideologies to disguise the truth and their own paranoia. And the masses chimed in enthusiastically because they were unaware of the real motives, including those operative in their own biographies. The infantile revenge fantasies of individuals would be of no account if society did not regularly show such naive alacrity in helping to make them come true.

Naturally, my references to Schreber and his methods are not sufficient to explain the history of the Holocaust. Countless books have been written about it, but the enormity of those crimes still defies comprehension. Much more research needs to be done before we can even start to truly understand. Given what we know today, attempting to build an explanation around any one single factor would result in crass over--simplification.

It leaves too many other things out of account. Also, such a monocausal explanation might lead to an exoneration of the perpetrators, relieving them of their responsibility by declaring them sick. No upbringing, however cruel, is a license for murder. But blaming the whole thing on a defective genetic blueprint is just as unsatisfactory. Why should there have been so many people born 30 or 40 years before the Holocaust in Germany with such a fateful genetic disposition? I do not know of any gene researcher who would have tried to answer this question.

My references to the systematic humiliation of children around the turn of the century and the torture small infants were exposed to (tragically never recognized as such by the parents) seem to me, however, to be an important element within the complex concatenation of causes. Unfortunately it has yet to be given the attention it deserves. The reasons for this neglect are probably closely connected with the general taboo that has been imposed on the subject of childhood. But for quite hard--headed pragmatic reasons, notably a concern for the future, it is important to break with this taboo and venture onto this largely unexplored territory.

The total neglect or trivialization of the childhood factor operative in the context of violence and the way it evolves in early infancy sometimes leads to explanations that are not only unconvincing and abortive but actively deflect attention away from the genuine roots of violence. The abstract term "anti--Semitism" contains an infinite number of meanings and frequently only serves to blur the complicated psychological processes involved, processes that need to be identified and called by name. Only in this way can we hope to change anything.

In my view, a close comparison of parenting methods today and in the past can bring about such a change. It can open up new vistas and encourage the formation of new and healthier structures in raising children. Many new enlightening books on parent--child relations are instances of concrete help for parents in incorporating the information at our disposal into the practice of childrearing. Parents who are able to integrate this new information are likely to find it easier to respect, encourage, understand and love their children and to learn from them.

But working toward a better, more aware future cannot be done in isolation from the ongoing attempt to understand our history in all its facets, for us as individuals and as society. The work started by Lloyd deMause and continued by him and other psychohistorians is to my knowledge the first systematic research in this direction. The history of childrearing might be more illuminating than many others in illustrating the dangers for society at large attendant on willful ignorance about child development. The ongoing research on babies from birth to three might be helpful for eventually overcoming this ignorance. It may enable some historians to raise more frequently the question raised for the first time by Lloyd deMause: what does it feel like to be an abused infant, without any enlightened witness? Unfortunately, the early childhood of people who recently mercilessly killed in Rwanda has not yet become an issue for psychological or sociological investigation. But should empathic psychohistorians once become interested in finding out and describing the atmosphere of the first years of the killer's life, they could probably be able to explain some of the events that still seem inexplicable.

Child marriage is both a human rights violation and a barrier to development. It robs girls of their ability to reach their full potential and makes it harder for families, communities and countries to escape poverty.

To succeed in reducing poverty and achieving other development goals-especially improving the lives of women and children-ending child marriage must become a policy priority, both for governments and international donors.

Today 51 million girls ages 17 or younger in developing countries are married. If child marriage is left unchecked, an additional 1 00 million girls in developing countries will be married within the next decade-some before they reach age 10. That's 25,000 girls being married every day for the next 10 years.

The costs of doing nothing are high for both girls and communities. In some of the poorest countries, girls are not attending school because they are being prepared for early marriage. Of those attending school, many are forced to drop out because they are married off at a young age. Their friendships with peers often are restricted. And they cannot take advantage of economic opportunities-including those stemming from development assistance programs. Their health also is at risk because of early sexual activity and childbearing. And they have little or no access to quality health care services. Many child brides also experience domestic violence from spouses and their relatives.

The costs also are high for developing countries. Countries with high child marriage rates have high rates of maternal and child mortality, as well as extreme and persistent poverty.

Child marriage is a development problem that needs immediate attention. The practice is most common in sub-Saharan Africa and South Asia, but it also occurs at high rates in parts of Latin America and the Caribbean-including many countries supported by the President's Emergency Plan for AIDS Relief (PEPFAR) or the Millennium Challenge Account (MCA)-see related table, this page. The causes of child marriage are complex, varied and often interlinked. Socioeconomic factors such as poverty, family circumstances, a community's marriage customs and practices, and girls' lack of access to empowering options like education all play a role in whether girls marry too young.

- o *Poverty*: In some families, girls may be viewed as an economic burden. In these cases, marriage can be perceived as the best tool to alleviate the burden of having one more mouth to feed.
- o *Transfer of Wealth*: Dowry and bridewealth-which involve the exchange of money, livestock or other wealth from the bride's family to the groom's, or vice versa-often are determined by the age of the bride. Lower dowry costs or higher bridewealth gains for girls' families serve as a common incentive for marrying girls early.

- o *Custom*: Community customs regarding the appropriate age for marriage can exert a great deal of social pressure on parents to marry their daughters at young ages. In places where the custom is to marry daughters at age 9 or 10, a girl reaching her 15th or 16th birthday may be considered past the marriageable age. Parents often worry that if they don't marry their daughters according to social expectations, they will not be able to marry them at all.
- o *Protection*: For many parents, marriage is seen as a way to protect their daughters. Parents fear their daughters may become victims of violence or rape; at times girls must walk alone-sometimes long distances-to school or to collect firewood and water. And in some communities where virginity is prized and associated with family honor, parents want to protect their daughters from engaging in premarital sex.
- o *Ties that Bind*: Marriage in many communities serves as a means for strengthening economic, social and political ties between different families and communities. The early marriage of a daughter may help reinforce such a tie or establish a new bond that improves the standing of the family or community. It is not uncommon for young girls to be offered in marriage to a family that is known to own more land or livestock.
- o *Little Education and Few Options*: If no schooling or work is available, a young girl may get married based on her family's economic need or to secure her economic future. In some communities, young girls are withdrawn from school so they can marry.

Research shows that the younger girls are when they marry, the wider the age difference between husband and wife. Married girls often lack status and power within their marriages and households-especially when their spouse is significantly older. A wide spousal age gap increases the likelihood that girls will be isolated and experience domestic violence and health risks, including HIV infection. In sub-Saharan Africa, especially West Africa, a significant spousal age gap often is tied to the practice of polygamy-the marriage of one man to more than one woman. Large age gaps between spouses are more common in polygamous than monogamous unions because men tend to wait until they are older and can afford to have multiple wives; adolescent girls often are taken as a second or third wife.

PROTECTIVE OR RISKY?

Marriage to Older Men

Child marriage makes it harder for families, communities and countries to escape poverty. It erodes the health and well-being of girls and the overall welfare of communities. It also undercuts international efforts to fight poverty and HIV/AIDS, improve child health and survival, and support other international development initiatives, making billions of development assistance dollars less effective. Child Marriage Threatens the Effectiveness of Economic Growth Programs Girls who marry young are more likely to be poor and remain poor. Child marriage is most common among the poor and in rural communities.

In sub-Saharan Africa, the practice is twice as common among the poorest families (lower 40th percentile) as compared to the richest families (top 20th percentile). In certain countries, this income gap is even wider. A poorer woman in Senegal, for example, is more than four times as likely to be a child bride as her richer peers. Moreover, girls who marry young have less education and fewer economic opportunities, which greatly increases the chance that they-and their children-will remain poor. Child Marriage Undercuts Health and Nutrition Programs Girls who marry young experience greater health risks.

- o *Undernutrition and Malnutrition*: Early marriage is often followed by early pregnancy. Girls who are pregnant or lactating require more calories and nutrients compared to those who are not, and when this extra nutrition is not available, their nutritional status is compromised. Married girls who are thin and undernourished before becoming pregnant are particularly vulnerable to becoming malnourished during pregnancy. Young mothers also are less able to adequately care for their children, and this often compromises their children's nutritional status.
- o *Maternal Mortality*: Girls between the ages of 10 and 14 are five times more likely to die in pregnancy and childbirth than women ages 20 to 24; girls ages 15 to 19 are twice as likely to die.
- o *Infant Mortality*: The underdeveloped bodies of young girls can lead to complication in childbirth that can result in the death of the child (see related chart, page 5).
- o *Obstetric Fistula*: A 2003 study by the U.N. Population Fund and EngenderHealth of nine African countries found fistula patients to most often be poor young women, ages 15 to 20, many of whom reported having been married young. Obstetric fistula results when a young mother's vagina, bladder and/or rectum tear during childbirth, a condition that causes urine and feces leakage.
- o *HIV Infection*: The 2004 study, Early Marriage and HIV Risk in Sub-Saharan Africa by Shelley Clark,

found that in Kenya and Zambia being married increases a girl's chance of being HIV-positive by more than 75 percent over sexually active unmarried girls.

I am 14 years old.

I was promised into marriage at birth.

My husband is nearly twice my age.

I've dropped out of school.

I have no job opportunities.

I am hungry and there's little food to eat.

My husband and family pressure me to become pregnant and have children.

My chance of dying in childbirth or from related complications are much higher than average.

The chance of my child being healthy and surviving birth or infancy are much lower.

I am more likely to become infected with HIV.

I have few friends; my husband controls where

I can go and who I can see, and I often feel lonely.

Who Am I? A Child Bride

Child Marriage Impedes the Success of Education Programs

Child marriage often ends a girl's education. In Mali, 86 percent of married girls have received no education, and nine out of 10 married girls cannot read.

Child Marriage Violates the Human Rights of Women and Girls Married girls are more susceptible to domestic violence. ICRW research in India shows that women married as children were twice as likely to report being beaten, slapped or threatened by their husbands as women who were married as adults. They also were three times as likely to report being forced to have sex.

WHAT CAN POLICYMAKERS DO? END CHILD MARRIAGE

Countries like South Korea, Taiwan and Thailand have eliminated the practice of child marriage in little more than a generation. The marriage-age increase in these countries has been coupled with increases in the levels of education and economic opportunities for girls and young women as well as broader development success in terms of economic growth and improvements in health and welfare. Experience in these countries shows the close connection between later marriages and successful development investments.

The means for tackling the global problem of child marriage exist. They include programs that educate parents and young people about the effects of child marriage; improve girls' access to health care services; and provide girls better educational, nutritional and economic opportunities. Research shows that girls tend to marry later if they have higher levels of education and access to employment options.

Positive change also stems from efforts that mobilize communities and and equip them with information about the causes and consequences of child marriage. Community organizations, parents, and tribal and religious leaders in Ethiopia have mobilized-and continue to mobilize-to end the practice of child marriage in their communities. The Ethiopian government also recently amended the country's family law and penal code to outlaw marriage before the age of 18. Similar efforts are taking placing in communities throughout the developing world.

"Child marriage and the betrothal of girls and boys shall be prohibited and effective action, including legislation, shall be taken to specify the minimum age of marriage to be 18 years."

1990 AFRICAN CHARTER ON THE RIGHTS AND WELFARE OF THE CHILD

Prohibiting the marriage of girls and boys before they become adults has near universal consensus among governments. In Africa-one of the regions with the highest incidence of this practice-countries came together more than a decade ago to adopt the 1990 African Charter on the Rights and Welfare of the Child, which calls for states to take action to end child marriage. In fact, most developing countries are signatories to international agreements and conventions opposing child marriage and have laws setting a minimum age of marriage.

Despite such efforts, the legal age of marriage remains 16 in at least 15 countries, and 20 countries have no minimum age requirement. Many countries also allow early marriage with parental consent. Moreover, in a handful of countries the law allows a perpetrator of rape-including statutory rape of a minor-to be excused of his crime if he marries his victim. Even when legal protections exist, they may not be fully enforced and in some cases, traditional law overrides statutory law. The international consensus is that early marriage is harmful and should be prohibited. The Inter-African Committee on Traditional Practices Affecting the Health of Women and Children defines early marriage as "any marriage carried out below the age of 18 years, before the girl is physically, physiologically and psychologically ready to shoulder the responsibilities of marriage and childbearing."

An array of international instruments echoes this perspective. The 1948 Universal Declaration of Human Rights states that men and women of "full age" have the right to marry and have a family. It adds: "Marriage shall be entered into only with the free and full consent of the intending spouses:"

Understanding the Legal Environment of Child Marriage

The potential for eliminating child marriage through community mobilization is great. Other harmful traditional practices have been eradicated through community action. For example, over the past decade the practice of female genital cutting has been nearly eliminated in some African settings because local communities and international development organizations worked together to generate the necessary support.

The United States through its diplomacy and development assistance programs is well-placed to demonstrate leadership on the issue of child marriage. Specifically, U.S. development assistance programs can further efforts to:

- o Increase access to, enrollment in and completion of both primary and secondary education by girls-both married and unmarried.
- o Provide girls and young women with safe employment opportunities outside of the home.
- o Support and expand nutrition and immunization programs for young mothers and children.
- o Support and expand access to family planning services and information for both married and unmarried youth.
- o Increase women's and girls' access to health care services by providing funding for medical outreach centers in rural communities, modern equipment and supplies, emergency obstetrics care and the medical transportation needs of rural families.

- o Increase opportunities for local communities to train and retain skilled health care workers, including midwives.
- o Educate parents and young people about their rights, laws, international norms and the benefits of delaying marriage.
- o Include the special needs of young married girls in HIV/AIDS prevention, care, testing and treatment programs.
- o Support programs to end violence against women.
- o Support additional research on child marriage, its causes and solutions.

Child marriage is a development problem that must not be ignored. Addressing its causes and providing solutions for its consequences should be part of any compassionate development agenda. Ending child marriage not only will protect girls and ensure a better future for them and their families, it also will ensure stronger and healthier families and communities.

6

CHILD MARRIAGE: A VIOLATION OF HUMAN RIGHTS

Child marriage is a violation of human rights. WPF and IHEU therefore urge all governments to end child marriage: a practice in which the parents of a child arrange a marriage with another child or an adult. In most cases young girls get married off to significantly older men when they are still children. Child marriages must be viewed within a context of force and coercion, involving pressure and emotional blackmail, and children that lack the choice or capacity to give their full consent. Child marriage must therefore always be considered forced marriage because valid consent is absent-and often considered unnecessary.

Child marriage is common practice in Niger, Chad, Mali, Bangladesh, Guinea, Burkina Faso, Central African Republic, Mozambique, Nepal, Uganda and Cameroon, where over 50% of girls are married by the age of 18. More than 30% of girls are married by the age of 18 in another eighteen countries, mostly in Asia and Africa. Poverty, protection of girls, fear of loss of virginity before marriage and related family honour, and the provision of stability during unstable social periods are suggested as significant factors in determining a girl's risk of becoming married as a child. Statistics show that child marriage is most common among the poorest groups in society.

PHYSICAL, SOCIAL AND PSYCHOLOGICAL CONSEQUENCES OF CHILD MARRIAGE

Young girls who get married will most likely be forced into having sexual intercourse with their, usually much older, husbands. This has severe negative health consequences as the girl is often not psychologically, physically and sexually mature. Child brides are likely to become pregnant at an early age and there is a strong correlation between the age of a mother and maternal mortality and morbidity. Girls aged 10-14 are five times more likely to die in pregnancy or childbirth than women aged 20-24 and girls aged 15-19 are twice as likely to die.

The body of a young girl is not yet ready for pregnancy and childbirth, which leads to complications such as obstructed labour and obstetric fistula. Obstetric fistula can also be caused by the early sexual relations associated with child marriage, which take place sometimes even before menarche. Good prenatal care reduces the risk of childbirth complications, but in many instances, due to their limited autonomy or freedom of movement, young wives have no access to health services, which aggravates the risks of maternal complications and mortality for pregnant adolescents. Because young girls are not ready for the responsibilities and roles of being a wife, sexual partner and a mother, child marriage has a serious negative impact on their psychological well-being and personal development.

On top of pregnancy-related complications, young married girls are also at high risk of contracting HIV/AIDS. Girls are disproportionately affected by HIV/AIDS as compared to boys due to physical and social factors. Young married girls are even at higher risk because their older husbands may already be infected in previous sexual relationships. Furthermore, the age difference between the girl and the husband and her low economic status make it almost impossible for the girl to negotiate safe sex or demand fidelity. Girls and women who are married younger, especially when married as children, are more likely to experience domestic violence and to believe that it is justified for a man to beat his wife. In addition, child brides are least likely to take action against this abuse. Domestic violence seriously endangers the physical and mental health of women and girls and can even put their lives at risk.

Gender inequality is both a cause as well as a consequence of child marriage. Child brides usually have lower levels of education than girls who get married at an older age. Education is therefore seen as a way to prevent child marriages. Once a girl is married, she experiences a lack of autonomy to make personal decisions about her life. Early marriage, together with its relation to low levels of education, high levels of violence and abuse, severe health risks and harmful power dynamics, results in increased vulnerability to poverty for girls and young women.

HUMAN RIGHTS VIOLATION

Child marriage is a violation of human rights and is prohibited by a number of international conventions and other instruments. Nonetheless, it is estimated that in the next ten years more than 100 million girls are likely to be married before the age of 18. The Universal Declaration of Human Rights (1948) states that men and women of full age are entitled to equal rights as to marriage, during marriage and at its dissolution. Marriage shall be entered into only with the free and full consent of the intending parties. The Convention on Consent to Marriage, Minimum Age for Marriage and Registration of Marriages (1964) says that no marriage shall be legally entered into without the full and free consent of both parties. States should specify a minimum age for marriage (not less than 15 years) and all marriages should be registered by the competent authority. The Convention on the Elimination of All Forms of Discrimination of Women (1979) states that the betrothal and the marriage of a child shall have no legal effect, and all necessary action, including legislation, should be taken to specify a minimum age for marriage and to make the registration of marriages in an official registry compulsory. In their general recommendations of 1994, the Committee considers that the minimum age for marriage should be 18 years for both men and women.

The African Charter on the Rights and Welfare of the Child (1990) prohibits child marriage and the betrothal of girls and boys. Effective action, including legislation, should be taken to specify the minimum age of marriage to be 18 years.

Concrete Action Points

We call on all governments to take all necessary action to end child marriage by:

- o The full implementation of the above mentioned Human Rights Conventions
- o Adopting a clear and unambiguous position on child and forced marriages and rectifying the legislative loopholes between religious, customary and civil marriages (Ouagadougou Declaration on Child Marriage, October 2003)
- o Introducing laws to raise the legal age of marriage to 18 years, as agreed in the African Charter on the Rights and Welfare of the Child
- o Raising the awareness of all stakeholders, including parents, on the negative impacts of child marriage
- o Creating safety nets for girls and young women who escape a forced, and often violent, marriage
- o Creating and maintaining birth, death and marriage data registries with full national coverage in all

countries as recommended in the Pinheiro report on violence against children (2006)

- o Promoting and protecting the sexual and reproductive health and rights of girls and young women, through legislation, availability of services and information and community outreach
- o Promoting gender equality and the right of girls and young women to education

We urge governments to include a strong statement against child marriage in the outcome documents and resolutions of the CSW's 51st session on 'The elimination of all forms of discrimination and violence against the girl child'. We also urge the Commission on the Status of Women to take this statement to the forthcoming review of the Children's Summit in April 2007.

WOMEN'S STATUS AND MARRIAGE PATTERNS IN INDIA

Women in India marry and begin childbearing at young ages. About 5 percent of girls between the ages of 10 and 14, slightly over 35 percent of adolescent women between the ages of 15 and 19 and about 82 percent of young women between the ages of 20 and 24 are married in India (Census of India, 1991). And because the majority of Indian births occur within marriage, unraveling issues surrounding women's status and marriage patterns is critical for gaining a deeper understanding of the basic family demography of India and the decision-making power of women within marriages.

Data from the 1998-1999 National Family Health Survey (NFHS2) of India are used in this paper to examine marriage patterns and their correlates for a sample of 64,855 once-married women between the ages of 25 and 49. We first describe the basic characteristics of marriage for the sample and then relate several measures of women's status to different dimensions of marriage: age at marriage, child marriage, late marriage, age difference between spouses, and education difference between spouses. The net effects of women's age, language, caste, standard of living, childhood residence, literacy status, and stated son preference on these dimensions of marriage are examined.

Since 1978 the legal age at marriage in India is 18 for women, yet 66 percent of the women in the sample were married before age 18. The mean age at marriage for the sample is 16.1 years, but varies from a low of 15.4 years in the north and northwestern regions of India, to a high of 18.3 years in the Himalayan hill states. We find that 34 percent of women in the sample were married as children (age 14 and younger). However, there is considerable regional variation in the sample with the northern region showing 39 percent of women married at age 14 or younger, while the hill states show only 13 percent of women married as children. Late marriages (ages 25 and older) represent only 4 percent nationally and range from 2 percent in the north and east to 9 percent in the hill states.

The average educational difference between spouses is 2.6 years with noticeable regional variation. The hill states have an educational difference between spouses of 1.7 years. In the north, the average educational difference between spouses is 3.4 years. For a smaller sample of women (59,860) we find an average age difference between spouses of 6.1 years.

Results from the regression analysis of age at marriage show that being literate and having a literate partner, and having grown up in an urban area have positive effects on age at marriage. Women's age, Hindi speakers (compared to non-Hindi speakers), and Hindus and Muslims (compared to other religions), members of a scheduled caste or tribe (compared to other castes), and low and medium standards of living (compared to high), as well as stated son preference, all have negative effects on age at marriage. Results from logistic regression analysis show that older women, Hindi speakers, Hindus and Muslims, those from low or medium economic class levels, and those with son preference are more likely than others to have married as a child (age 14 or younger). Women who are literate, have literate partners, and those who grew up in urban areas are less likely to have married as children. Caste or tribal membership does not have a significant effect on child marriage.

Next, we report results from the regression analysis of age difference between spouses. Older women, Hindus and Muslims, and those from low or medium standards of living have greater age difference from spouses. However, being literate or having a literate husband, Hindi speakers, and being a member of a scheduled caste or tribe, growing up in an urban area, and having a stated son preference all negatively affect age difference between spouses.

Results from regression analysis also show that women's age, husband's literacy, Hindi speakers, Hindus and Muslims, those from a scheduled caste or tribe, and son preference have positive effects on education difference between spouses. Female literacy, low or medium standard of living, and growing up in an urban area have negative effects on education difference between spouses. In the final paper we will also report findings relating women's status and marriage patterns to their household decision making. The net effects of measures of women's status, along with age at marriage, and age and education difference between spouses, on the relative power and freedom women have to make household and other decisions will also be examined. These decisions are about cooking, health care, purchases, going to market, visiting relatives and friends, or setting aside money.

HOW TO END CHILD MARRIAGE

Girls who marry as children are often more susceptible to the health risks associated with early sexual initiation and childbearing, including HIV and obstetric fistula. Lacking status and power, these girls are often subjected to domestic violence, sexual abuse and social isolation. And early marriage almost always deprives girls of their education or meaningful work, which contributes to persistent poverty. Child Marriage perpetuates an unrelenting cycle of gender inequality, sickness and poverty. Its consequences ripple through the world's poorest regions devastating the lives of girls, their families and their communities. Despite nearly universal condemnation, this harmful tradition thrives: 51 million girls are married. If nothing changes, another 100 million girls will be married within the decade. The international community recognizes child marriage as a serious development problem, but growing awareness has not led to committed, coordinated action against the practice.

Political commitment at the highest levels can help achieve a world where girls and women are healthy, safe and empowered. Decision makers, development experts and donors must now turn their attention to what can be done to prevent girls from marrying too early and protect those who are already married. The good news is that innovative community-based efforts appear to be providing viable alternatives to early marriage. These promising interventions could have a significant impact on reducing child marriage, if more resources are made available to rigorously evaluate what is working and scale up successful programs. This policy brief outlines what we can and should be doing to end child marriage: changing harmful cultural norms, supporting community programs, maximizing foreign assistance, increasing access to girls' education, providing young women with economic opportunities, addressing the unique needs of child brides and evaluating programs to determine what works.

TRANSFORM HARMFUL CULTURAL NORMS

Child marriage is deeply embedded in cultural traditions, which can be difficult to change. However, as the campaign against female genital cutting demonstrates, community mobilization can be effective in initiating behavior change and discouraging harmful practices. Many indigenous communities already are taking action to end child marriage. A program scan conducted by the International Center for Research on Women (ICRW) found these community-based interventions are working to reduce early marriage with multifaceted programs that educate families and community members on the dangers of child marriage, provide girls with education and life skills, and offer legal services, among other activities.

Support and Scale Up Community Programs

Grassroots efforts, coupled with national policies that prohibit child marriage, signal a desire among governments and local communities to end the practice. Yet many of these countries lack the resources to implement, coordinate and expand efforts to reduce early marriage. ICRW's Web-based program scan found only 69 programs addressing child marriage. These programs, of various sizes and resources, are missing from areas where the needs are greatest. In six of the 20 countries with the highest prevalence of child marriage, no programs were found. Aside from ICRW's program scan, there is no known effort to compile information on approaches to reduce early marriage. More information on existing programs can help fill gaps in understanding the complexities of child marriage prevention and identify best practices for replication and scaling up. Policy-makers and program planners could also benefit from improved coordination across countries to share program and advocacy designs, experiences and lessons from their work to delay marriage.

Maximize Aid Dollars

The negative consequences of child marriage impede international development efforts. The top 20 "hot spot" countries for child marriage also have some of the highest rates of maternal and child mortality as well as extreme and persistent poverty. International donors could improve the effectiveness of aid dollars by integrating child marriage prevention initiatives into existing development initiatives. The United States, for example, already funds many programs worldwide to reduce poverty; ensure the survival and health of infants, children and mothers; provide access to voluntary family planning; fight AIDS; and invest in girls' education. All of these are undermined by the practice of child marriage.

Increase Access to Girls' Education

Research suggests programs that provide or increase access to education for girls are crucial to delaying marriage. Girls with eight or more years of schooling are less likely to marry early than girls with zero to three years of education. But primary education is not enough. Women are more likely to control their own destinies and effect change in their communities when they have higher levels of education. All levels of education must be made more accessible to girls so that more girls will be enrolled and retained. Parents and community leaders also need to be sensitized to support girls in school. And married girls, too, need to be encouraged to continue their education.

Provide Economic Opportunities for Young Women

Child marriage is inextricably linked to poverty, and families' economic status strongly indicates whether their daughters will be married early. Child brides have less access to schooling and paid work. Cut off from educational and economic opportunities, girls who marry young are more likely to be poor and remain poor. Eliminating child marriage could contribute to broad efforts to reduce long-term poverty. In the short term, targeted incentives for postponing marriage into adulthood and providing economic opportunities for unmarried girls after they finish school can help delay marriage. These livelihood opportunities include skills training, microcredit or savings clubs, and jobs and job placement services. Policy-makers and program planners should also consider ways to make it easier for families to afford education fees and send girls to school. Expanding opportunities for girls and young women can help change social norms that view marriage as their only option, particularly in cultures where bride price and dowry are common.

Support the Needs of Child Brides

Prevention is the primary focus of child marriage interventions, but policy-makers and program planners must not overlook the millions of girls who have already married early and who bear children while still children themselves. To guard against the increased health risks, programs focused on child marriage should support child brides and their families by promoting earlier and more frequent use of family planning, HIV/AIDS and maternal health services.

Adolescent girls face a greater risk of sexual and reproductive health problems than adult women, but they are less likely to seek health services, often because of their low status in the marital home and community. ICRW research on adolescent reproductive health found that it is possible to change social taboos and gender norms that restrict young people's access to and use of health services in a relatively short period of time by involving family elders, peers and health care staff. Married girls also need educational and economic opportunities to help break the cycle of inequality, illiteracy, illness and poverty that perpetuates child marriage. Educated women have more opportunities to improve their own well-being and that of their family than women without an education. Research shows that the education of girls and mothers leads to sustained increases in educational attainment from one generation to the next. Also, improving women's access to paid work is critical to the survival and security of poor households and an important way to lift these households out of poverty. Evaluate Programs to Determine What Works Some community-based approaches to delaying marriage appear to be working, but few programs are evaluated for impact, making it difficult to determine whether and how age of marriage was increased. Donors should support monitoring and evaluation components of programs because these funds help ensure programs are achieving their intended results. Ongoing monitoring and evaluation can be contained to as little as 20 percent of total program costs, an investment that ensures programs can be adjusted for effectiveness and replicated when successful.

Why the Youngest Girls are Vulnerable

Younger girls are particularly vulnerable to being married to men who are significantly older or men who have multiple wives. Wide spousal age gaps are far more customary in countries with high rates of child marriage than in countries with lower rates. Large age differences between husband and wife may intensify a young bride's lower status and lack of power, increasing the likelihood that she will experience violence and health risks, including HIV. ICRW research shows that in countries with high prevalence, child marriage first begins to increase significantly at a "tipping point" age. Prevention efforts should target young girls before they reach the tipping point. These may include promoting primary education for girls and educating families and communities on the dangers of early marriage for young girls.

WHAT WE KNOW ABOUT THE RISK AND PROTECTIVE FACTORS FOR CHILD MARRIAGE

Understanding and addressing the factors that influence whether a girl will be married early can help guide efforts to reduce child marriage and mitigate its unwanted consequences. ICRW research found the following risk and protective factors.

Region: Cultural and socioeconomic factors that reinforce child marriage vary from region to region. Where a girl lives within a country may strongly influence whether she will marry early. For example, prevalence varies widely in India, where half of girls are married before 18. The highest rates are concentrated in five states: Madhya Pradesh at 73 percent, Andhra Pradesh at 71 percent, Rajasthan at 68 percent, Bihar at 67 percent and Uttar Pradesh at 64 percent. Similarly, in Ethiopia, almost half of early marriages are concentrated in four northern regions.

Poverty: Child marriage is most common in the world's poorest countries and among the poorest households. Girls living in poor households are almost twice as likely as girls from wealthier homes to marry before 18. Although families have different motivations for marrying their daughters early, girls are sometimes seen as an economic burden that can be relieved through marriage.

Education

Girls in developing countries often must overcome substantial obstacles in accessing educational opportunities. Research shows that low levels of education greatly increase the risk that a girl will marry as a child. Higher levels of education—particularly attending secondary school—can protect girls from early marriage. In Mozambique, nearly 60 percent of girls with no education are married by 18, compared to 10 percent of girls with secondary schooling and less than 1 percent with higher education. Research shows that schooling helps girls develop aspirations and gives them skills to negotiate who and when they will marry.

Top 20 "Hot Spot" Countries for Child Marriage

Ranking	Country	Percent Married Younger than 18
1	Niger	76.6
2	Chad	71.5
3	Bangladesh	68.7
4	Mali	65.4
5	Guinea	64.5
6	Central African Republic	57.0
7	Nepal	56.1
8	Mozambique	55.9
9	Uganda	54.1
10	Burkina Faso	51.9
11	India	50.0
12	Ethiopia	49.1
13	Liberia	48.4
13	Yemen	48.4
15	Cameroon	47.2
16	Eritrea	47.0
17	Malawi	46.9
18	Nicaragua	43.3
18	Nigeria	43.3
20	Zambia	42.1

Source: Demographic Health Survey (DHS) Data

THE CHILD MARRIAGE RESTRIANT ACT, 1929

An Act to restrain the solemnization of child marriages Whereas it is expedient to restrain the solemnization of child marriages; It is hereby enacted as follows:

Comments

Preamble-Use of.-It is true that the preamble and the aims and objects cannot be used for interpreting the statute. The preamble as well as the aims and objects of the Act can be used for limited purpose of ascertaining the conditions prevailing at the time of legislation and for finding out the purpose of the enactment by furnishing valuable historical material.

- Object and reasons of the Act.-The objects and reasons of the Act are to be taken into consideration in interpreting the provisions of the Statute and not the debates in Parliament on the Bill.
- Intention of Legislature.-In Prithvi Pal Singh Bedi v. Union of India, it was held that literal meaning of the statute must be adhered to when there is no absurdity in ascertaining the legislative intendment and for that purpose the broad feature of the Act can be looked into.
- Principle of "noscitur a sociis"-Application of.-Where two constructions are possible, that which would be more conducive to reason and justice is to be preferred by applying the principle of noscitur a sociis.
- Punctuation marks-Effects.-It is well known that punctuation marks by themselves do not control the meaning of a statute when its meaning is otherwise obvious.
- Words, clear, intelligible and unambiguous-Must be given effect to.-If the language of the statute is clear and intelligible and does not admit of two meanings, effect must be given to the words used and thus the intention of the Legislature must be carried out.
- Mandatory rule and directory rule-Difference.-The difference between a mandatory rule and a directory

rule is that while the former must be strictly observed, in the case of the latter, substantial compliance may be sufficient to achieve the object regarding which the rule is enacted. Certain broad propositions which can be deduced from several decisions of courts regarding the rules of construction that should be followed in determining whether a provision of law is directory or mandatory may be summarized thus:

- The fact that the statute uses the word "shall" while laying down a duty is not conclusive on the question whether it is a mandatory or directory provision. In order to find out the true character of the legislation the Court has to ascertain the object which the provision of law in question is to sub serve and its design and the context in which it is enacted. It the object of law is to be defeated by non-compliance with it, it has to be regarded as mandatory. But where a provision of law relates to the performance of any public duty and the invalidation of any act done in disregard of that provision causes serious prejudice to those for whose benefit it is enacted and at the same time who have no control over the performance of the duty, such provision should be treated as a directory one.
- Where, however, a provision of law prescribes that a certain act has to be done in a particular manner by a person in order to acquire a right and it is coupled with another provision which confers an immunity on another when such act is not done in that manner, the former has to be regarded as a mandatory one. A procedural rule ordinarily should not be construed as mandatory if the defect in the act done in pursuance of it can be cured by permitting appropriate rectification to be carried out at a subsequent stage unless by according such permission

to rectify the error later on, another rule would be contravened. Whenever a statute prescribes that a particular act is to be done in a particular manner and also lays down that a failure to comply with the said requirement leads to a specific consequences, it would be difficult to hold that the requirement is not mandatory and the specified consequence should not follow.

Interpretation must further and not frustrate the object of a statute. Interpretation of a statute, contextual or otherwise must further and not frustrate the object of the statute. Short title, extent and commencement.-

(1) This Act may be called the Child Marriage Restraint Act, 1929.

(2) It extends to the whole of India [except the State of Jammu and Kashmir] and it applies as also to all citizens of India without and beyond India: [Provided that nothing contained in this Act shall apply to the Renoncants of the Union territory of Pondicherry.]

(3) It shall come into force on the 1st day of April, 1930. Definitions.-In this Act, unless there is anything repugnant in the subject or context,-

(a) "child" means a person who, if a male, has not completed twenty-one years of age, and if a female, has not completed eighteen years of age;

(b) "child marriage" means a marriage to which either of the contracting parties is a child;

(c) "contracting party" to a marriage means either of the parties whose marriage is or is about to be thereby solemnized; and

(d) "minor" means a person of either sex who is under eighteen years of age.

Punishment for male adult below twenty-one years of age marrying a child.-Whoever, being a male above eighteen years of age and below twenty-one, contracts a child-marriage shall be punishable with simple imprisonment which may extend to fifteen days, or with fine which may extend to one thousand rupees, or with both.

Comment : Penal provisions-Interpretation.-The provision authorizing confiscation is a drastic one. In regard to such a provision it is well accepted that court should place construction which is in favour of the subject. Where the conjunction used is "or" unless there are compelling reasons to read "or" as "and" it is well settled that any word should be given its natural meaning. If it was intended that both the conditions must be satisfied there was no difficulty for the Legislature to use the expression "and" instead of "or". Punishment for male adult above twenty-one years of age marrying a child.-Whoever, being a male above twenty-one years of age, contracts a child marriage shall be punishable with simple imprisonment which may extend to three months and shall also be liable to fine.

Comment : Whoever-Meaning of.-According to the Shorter Oxford English Dictionary, Vol. 2, p. 2543, "whoever" means "any one who, any who". The meaning given in Webster Comprehensive Dictionary, International Ed., Vol.2 at p. 1437 is "any one without exception any person who". Punishment for solemnizing a child marriage.-Whoever performs, conducts or directs any child marriage shall be punishable with simple imprisonment which may extend to three months and also be liable to fine, unless he proves that he had reason to believe that the marriage was not a child marriage.

Comment : If marriage of Hindu male below eighteen years of age or female below fifteen years of age is invalid or illegal. The marriage of Hindu male below eighteen years of age with a Hindu girl of fifteen years of age is not invalidated or rendered illegal by the force of the Child Marriage Restraint- Act of 1929. It will remain a valid marriage binding under the Hindu Law if otherwise performed under any recognized form of Hindu La. It would be seen that the Child Marriage Restraint Act only restrains a marriage of minors and that is its Objective, but does not prohibit marriage rendering it illegal or invalid. It punishes those persons who arrange that marriage and actively participate in celebrating it.

The minor spouses who get married are not punished under the Act. Once it be held that the marriage itself is not illegal or invalid under the Child Marriage Restraint Act, 1929, then a debt incurred by the major members of the family for marrying a minor member of the family will not be for an illegal purpose as the marriage is legal and the debt is incurred for the marriage. It may be that the debt is incurred for the marriage. It may be that the consequence under the law would be that the major members be punished for their act in making arrangements for celebration of the marriage.

"May" and "shall".-The word "may" implies what is optional, but it should in some context in which it appears, mean "must". There is an element of compulsion. It is power coupled with a duty. In Maxwell on Interpretation of Statutes, 11 th Ed., p. 31, the principle is stated thus: "Statutes which authorize persons to do acts for the benefit of others, or, as is sometimes said, for the public good or the advancement of justice, have often given rise to controversy when conferring the authority in terms simply enabling and not mandatory. In enacting that they 'may' or 'shall' 'if they think fit', or 'shall have power' or that 'it shall be lawful' for them to do such acts, a statute appears to use the language of mere permission but it has been so often decided as to have become an axiom that in such cases such expressions may have to say the least a compulsory force, and so would seem to be modified by judicial exposition." The word "may" even if it was prima facie enabling, the Legislature may use it in the sense or "must" or "shall". Punishment for parent or guardian concerned in a child marriage.

(1) Where a minor contracts a child marriage, any person having charge of the minor, whether as parent or guardian or in any other capacity, lawful or solemnized, or negligently fails to prevent it from being solemnized, shall be punishable with simple imprisonment which may extend to three months and shall also be liable to fine:

Provided that no woman shall be punishable with imprisonment.

(2) For the purposes of this section, it shall be presumed, unless and until the contrary is proved, that where a minor has contracted a child marriage, the person having charge of such minor has negligently failed to prevent the marriage from being solemnized.

State Amendment

Gujarat.-After Sec. 6 of the principal Act the following section shall be inserted namely: Offences to be cognizable.-Notwithstanding anything contained in the Code of Criminal Procedure, 1898 (V of 1898), now new Code of 1973 (2 of 1974), an offence punishable under this Act shall be deemed to be a cognizable offence within the meaning of the Code.

Comment : Family.-The word "family" has to be given not a restricted but a wider meaning so as to include not only the head of the family but all members or descendants from the common ancestors who are actually living with the same head. The term "family" must always be liberally and broadly construed so as to include near relations of the head of the family. [7. Offences to be cognizable for certain purposes.-The Code of Criminal Procedure, 1973 (2 of 1974), shall apply to offences under this Act as if they were cognizable offences-(a) for the purpose of investigation of such offences; and (b) for the purpose of matters other than (i) matters referred to in Sec. 42 of that Code, and (ii) the arrest of a person without a warrant or without an order of a Magistrate.]

Jurisdiction under this Act.-Notwithstanding anything contained in Sec. 190 of the [Code of Criminal Procedure, 1973 (2 of 1974)), no court other than that of a 3[Metropolitan Magistrate or a Judicial Magistrate of the first class] shall take cognizance of, or try, any offence under this Act.

Comment : Offences under the Act cannot be tried by any Court other than the Courts referred therein.-There is an express prohibition under Sec. 8 of the Child Court other than the Courts referred to therein. Even any other Court cannot take cognizance of such offences. In view of this express prohibition in the special law which has an overriding effect, it is evident that even though the committing Magistrate has committed the accused to stand their trial, for offences under the Penal Code, which are triable by the Sessions Court, will not have jurisdiction to try these offences under the Act. The reason underlying it is that there is an express prohibition in special law which has got overriding effect over the provisions of general law.

Mode of taking cognizance of offences.-No Court shall take cognizance of any offence under this Act after the expiry of one year from the date on which the offence is alleged to have been committed. Preliminary inquiries into offences.-Any Court, on receipt of a complaint of an offence of which it is authorized to take cognizance, shall, unless it dismisses the complaint under Sec. 203 of the [Code of Criminal Procedure, 1973 (2 of 1974)], either itself make an inquiry under Sec. 202 of that Code or direct a Magistrate subordinate to it to make such inquiry.

Comment : Power vested in Magistrate to postpone issue of process.-Any Magistrate on receipt of a complaint of an offence of which he is authorized to take cognizance may do one of the two things. (1) He may for reasons to be recorded in writing, if he thinks fit, postpone the Issue of process for compelling the attendance of the person complained against. The content of the power vested in the Magistrate to postpone the issue of process for compelling the attendance of the person complained against, would also cover the power of issuing process for compelling the attendance of the person complained against. (2) After doing one of these two things, the Magistrate may either enquire into the case himself or he can direct any Magistrate subordinate to him to make an enquiry only for the limited purpose of ascertaining the truth or falsehood of the complaint.

State Amendment

Gujarat.-Section 10 is deleted. Power to take security from complainant.-[Repealed by the Child Marriage Restraint (Amendment) Act, 1949 (41 of 1949), Sec. 7]. [Power to issue injunction prohibiting marriage in contravention of this Act.-

(1) Notwithstanding anything to the contrary contained in this Act, the Court may, if satisfied, from information laid before it through a complaint or otherwise that a child marriage in contravention of this Act has been arranged or is about to be solemnized, issue an injunction against any of the persons mentioned in Secs. 3, 4, 5 and 6 of this Act prohibiting such marriage.

(2) No injunction under sub-section (1) shall be issued against any person unless the Court has previously

given notice to such person, and has afforded him an opportunity to show cause against the issue of the injunction.

(3) The Court may either on its own motion or on the application of any person aggrieved, rescind or alter any order made under sub-section (1).

(4) Where such an application is received, the Court shall afford the applicant an early opportunity of appearing before it either in person or by pleader; and if the Court rejects the application wholly or in part, it shall record in writing its reasons, for so doing.

(5) Whoever knowing that an injunction has been issued against him under sub-section (1) of this section disobeys such injunction shall be punished with imprisonment of either description for a term which may extend to three months, or with fine which may extend to one thousand rupees, or with both: Provided that no woman shall be punishable with imprisonment.]

State Amendment

Gujarat.-After Sec. 12 of the principal Act the following sections shall be added, namely: Child Marriage Prevention Officer.-

(1) The State Government may, by notification in the official Gazette, appoint for the whole State or for such part thereof as may be specified in that notification, an officer to be known as Child Marriage Prevention Officer.

(2) It shall be the duty of the Child Marriage Prevention Officer-

(i) to prevent marriages being performed in contravention of the provisions of this Act by taking such action under this Act as he deems fit;

(ii) to collect evidence for the effective prosecutions of persons contravening provisions of this Act; and

(iii) to discharge such other functions as may be assigned to him by the State Government.

(3) The State Government may, by notification in he official Gazette, invest the Child Marriage Prevention Officer with such powers of a police officer as maybe specified in the notification and the Child Marriage Prevention Officer shall exercise his powers subject to such limitation and conditions as may be specified in the notification.

(4) The State Government may associate with each Child Marriage Prevention Officer a non-official advisory body consisting of not more than five social welfare workers, of whom at least two shall be women workers known in the area within the jurisdiction of the officer for the purposes of advising and assisting him in the performance of his functions under this Act.

(5) The terms and conditions of appointment of persons on the advisory body shall be such as may be prescribed by rules. 13-A. Officer appointed under the Act to be public servant.-The Child Marriage Prevention Officer appointed under Sec. 13 shall be deemed to be a public servant within the meaning of Sec. 21 of the Indian Penal Code (XLV of 1860).

Protection of action taken in good faith.-No suit, prosecution or other legal proceedings shall lie against the Child Marriage Prevention Officer appointed under this Act in respect of anything in good faith done or intended to be done in pursuance of this Act or of any rules or orders made thereunder.

Power to make rules.-

(1) The State Government may, by notification in the official Gazette, māke rules, for the purposes of carrying out the provisions of this Act.

(2) In particular and without prejudice to the generality of the foregoing provision, such rules may provide for all matters expressly required or allowed by this Act to be prescribed by rules.

(3) The power to make rules conferred by this section is subject to the condition of the rules made after previous publication.

(4) All rules made under this section shall be laid for nor less than thirty days before the State Legislature as soon as possible after they are made, and shall be subject to rescission by the State Legislature or to such modifications as the State Legislature may make during the session in which they are so laid or the session immediately following.

(5) Any rescission or modification so made by the State Legislature shall be punished in the official Gazette and shall thereupon shall take effect." Other Measures to Prevent Child Marriages: Apart from the implementation of the Child Marriage Restraint Act, the Department has taken the following measures to prevent Child Marriages:-All the Programme Officers (ICDS) in the districts have been given instructions to keep a watch on child marriages and report such cases to District Administration and appropriate authorities for taking action as per Child Marriage Restraint Act.

Director Panchayats, State Women Commission all the Deputy Commissioners and Superintendents of Police and Programme Officers have been circulated instructions received from National Commission for women to launch

Bal Vivah Virodh Abhiyan. Department has also requested Dowry Prohibition Officers to keep vigial on Akha Teej & during marriage season to prevent child marriage. Department has also instructed Programme Officers / Child Development Project Officers to be vigilant regarding child marriages during marriage season.

Instructions issued to all the Programme Officers to bring provisions of the Child Marriage Restraint Act to the notice of all Sarpanches as well as Pandits, Granthis and Molvees who get the marriages solemnized through a letter to them. The format of letter to be sent by all Child Development Project Officers to above mentioned persons periodically given in annexure. Directions given by the Hon'ble Supreme Court in Writ Petition Civil No. 212 of 2003 conveyed to all Superintendents of Police in the State, Secretary Home Department, director General Health Department, Director Primary / Higher Education, Director Panchayat and Secretary, Revenue Department, Haryana to monitor the implementation of the Child Marriage Restraint Act, 1929 and to give wide publicity to the provisions of the Act to educate the public about it so that the menace of early child marriage which violates the provisions of the said act is fully taken care of. NGOs are being involved by organizing vocational / cultural activities for children through Education Department. Awareness against child marriages is being created through Public Relations Department, Haryana and Haryana State Social Welfare Advisory Board.

CHILD MARRIAGE: A SILENT TRAGEDY

Throughout the developing world, millions of girls are married off to virtual strangers while they are still just children. Some are as young as six or seven years old when they are married. The girls themselves rarely have any say in the matter. Many do not even know or fully understand what is planned for them until they arrive at their husband's home. In families with limited resources, child marriage is often considered a way to provide for a daughter's future. Poor families have few resources to support more healthy alternatives for girls, while economic gains through marrying off a daughter may also motivate poor parents to choose this path.

Worldwide, 100 million girls will be married before the age of 18 in the next decade alone. In countries like Niger and Bangladesh, grinding poverty and adherence to tradition results in more than three out of every four girls being married off before they turn 18 (ICRW). Child marriage is a great threat to young girls, for health and other reasons:

- Child brides are often pressured to bear children themselves long before their bodies are fully developed. Combined with lack of power, lack of information, and reduced access to health services, it can be disastrous. Girls younger than 15 are five times more likely to die in childbirth than women in their 20s, and pregnancy is the leading cause of death worldwide for girls ages 15 to 19. Early childbearing can cause obstetric fistula (when a young mother's vagina, bladder and/or rectum tear during childbirth) a condition that causes urine and feces leakage, often resulting in ostracism.
- Adolescent childbirth is extremely dangerous for the infant, as well. Children born to young girls are far more likely to perish than are children born to older mothers.
- Young brides are at higher risk for contracting HIV/AIDS. Girls are often married to significantly older men who are more likely to have contracted HIV in their lifetime. In sub-Saharan Africa, married girls have a notably greater risk of HIV infection than

sexually active single girls of the same age because married girls cannot abstain from sex or insist on the use of condoms. One study in Kenya and Zambia showed a young girl's married status increased the chances of her contracting HIV by an astounding 75 percent! (ICRW)

- After marriage, young girls' access to formal and even non-formal education is greatly limited because of domestic burdens, childbearing, and social norms that view marriage and schooling as incompatible. Removal from school is often the first thing that will happen to a child bride This is particularly tragic since primary education for girls is one of the most effective ways to fight the cycle of poverty and disease, reduce child death rates, improve nutrition, and promote democracy and development.
- Marriage also vastly reduces girls' access to resources like social support and autonomy. Young married girls have little power relative to their husbands and parents-in-law, leaving them extremely vulnerable to abuse. Girls who are married young are twice as likely to report being beaten and three times as likely to report being forced to have sex than women who marry after 18 years of age.

Promoting educational and economic opportunities for girls can reduce child marriage. Educating adolescent girls has been critical in increasing the age of marriage countries such as Indonesia, Sri Lanka, Taiwan, and Thailand. Working with parents and community leaders to increase these opportunities has delayed marriage for girls in parts of Kenya and Zimbabwe. Child marriage can be ended, but only with a more concerted effort to ensure the public, in all countries, are aware of the terrible toll child marriage takes on girls and their future children.

BIBLIOGRAPHY

Archavanitkul, K. and Havanon, N.: *Situation, Opportunities and Problems Encountered by Young Girls in Thai Society*, Bangkok, Terre des Hommes, 1990.

Bandman, B.: *Children's Right to Freedom, Care, and Enlightenment*, New York, Garland Publishing, 1999.

Banerjee, S.: *Child Labor in India*, London, The Anti-Slavery Society, 1979.

Bell, L.: *Good Girls/Bad Girls: Feminists and Sex Trade Workers Talk Face to Face*, Toronto: The Women's Press, 1987.

Bremner, H.: *Children and Youth: Social Problems and Social Policy Series*, New York, Arno Press, 1974.

Dodge, C.: *War, Violence, and Children in Uganda*, Oxford, Oxford University Press, 1987.

Ennew, J.: *Sexual Exploitation of Children*, Cambridge, Polity Press, 1986.

Fozzard, S.: *Surviving Violence: A Recovery Program for Children and Families*, Geneva, International Catholic child Bureau, 1995.

Greaney, Vincent: *Children - Needs and Rights*, New York, Irvington Publishers, 1985.

Harry, Patrinos: *The Policy Analysis of Child Marriage: A Comparative Study*, New York, St. Martin's Press, 1999.

Haspels, Nelien: *Action Against Child Marriage*, Washington, DC: Brookings Institution, 2000.

Hitchcock, K.: *Globalization, Child Labor, and Children's Rights*, Lincoln, Nebraska: Nebraskans for Peace, 2002.

Kent, G.: *Children in the International Political Economy*, New York, St. Martin's Press, 1995.

Kevin, Major: *Free the Children: A Young Man's Personal Crusade Against Child Labor*, New York, HarperCollins, 1998.

McCallin, M.: *The Psychological Well-being of Refugee Children: Research, Practice, and Policy Issues*, Geneva, International Catholic Child Bureau, 1996.

McIntosh, Robert: *Boys in the Pits: Child Labour in Coal Mines,* Montreal, McGill Queens University Press, 2000.

Nardinelli, Clark: *Child Labor and the Industrial Revolution,* Bloomington, Indiana University Press, 1990.

Philippe, A.: *Centuries of Childhood: A Social History of Family Life,* New York, Knopf, 1962.

Robert, H.: *Children and Youth: Social Problems and Social Policy Series,* New York, Arno Press, 1974.

Stein, R. Conrad: *The Story of Child Labor Laws (Cornerstones of Freedom),* Chicago, Children's Press, 1984.

West, Morris L: *Children of the Shadows; the True Story of the Street Urchins of Naples,* Garden City, N.Y., Doubleday, 1957.

White, B.: *Child Workers. Special Issue of Development and Change*, London, Sage Publications, 1982.

Woods, D.: *Child Soldiers: The Recruitment of Children in Armed Conflicts 1975-1989*. Eureka Springs, Center on War and the Child, 1990.

INDEX

□□□